One Small Valley

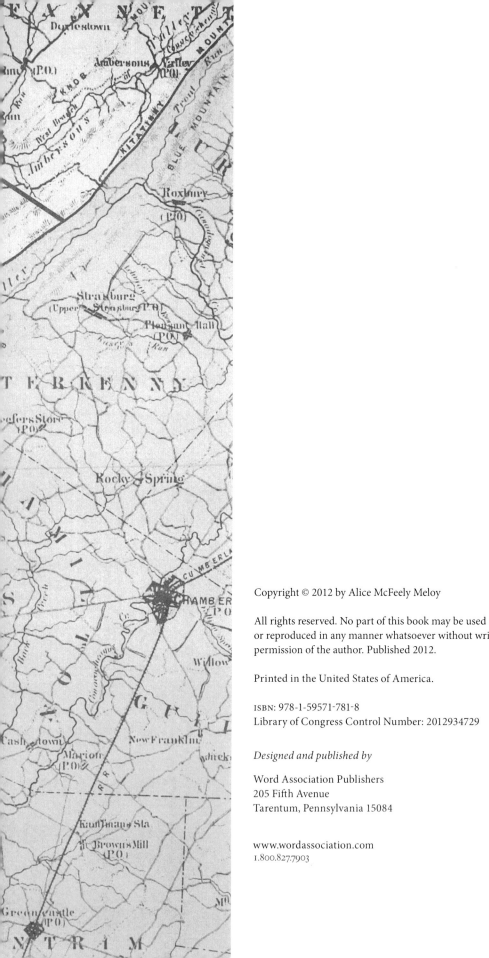

Printed in the United States of America.

ISBN: 978-1-59571-781-8
Library of Congress Control Number: 2012934729

Designed and published by

Word Association Publishers
205 Fifth Avenue
Tarentum, Pennsylvania 15084

www.wordassociation.com
1.800.827.7903

One Small Valley

Volume I
1734-1865

Alice McFeely Meloy

WORD ASSOCIATION PUBLISHERS
www.wordassociation.com
1.800.827.7903

Contents

. . . .

• •

PREFACE

*T*HE FOLLOWING STORY has been written in honor of our forefathers and mothers who settled in this small valley several centuries ago. They came seeking freedom, not from moral law, but to worship as they believed, to own a piece of ground they could call home and to gain an education for their children. Their voices still speak to us as we travel the hills, till the soil and worship in the churches they founded. We marvel at their courage, faith, ingenuity, work ethic and ability to find humor in adversity. What is even more astounding is that this small valley sent forth many sons and daughters who became leaders elsewhere, having been reared among these hills and ingrained with the values of our ancestors. This history is an attempt to share the story of a community, a people whom we have respected, loved and from whom we have learned.

One can never present a comprehensive or complete work of history. There are always missing pieces, different versions of the same event, variations of spelling where names are concerned and dates that differ. Sites of certain events from days when maps were not available cannot always be confirmed. In every chapter, there are questions that beg for further exploration. This is only a beginning. The quest for information never ends.

Sources include a number of books listed in the bibliography, as well as information from scraps of paper found in dusty trunks, old log books, diaries, programs, letters, and clipped newspaper articles without dates. Through the years, I have had the privilege of recording stories and taping interviews with friends who have now departed: Bess McCartney, Margaret Ferguson Stewart, Fred and Gail Walker Shearer, Bob and Eleanor Coons Crouse, Clyde Crouse, the McKim sisters, John Campbell, Bess Chilcoate, Dorothy Crouse, Herb Stewart, and my own grandmother, Mary "Addie" Robertson Ferguson.

I am also grateful for the generosity of my contemporaries who have read the manuscript, making valuable contributions: Dorothy Piper Medill, Tammy Bair Adams, Mary Vocke, Doris Campbell Crider, Edgar Greenawalt, Gerald Varner, and Wayne Campbell. Others have shared information: Tony Hockenberry, Harold Best, Bernice Crouse Harvey, Dick Klotz, Jane Stewart Atwell, and John Stewart. Visuals are important in any manuscript. I thank those who shared photographs and old postcards. Meg Meloy photographed old structures in existence today. Many photographs were taken years ago by my father, Herbert McFeely. Undoubtedly, I have missed some contributors. I apologize for the oversights that are inevitable with such a project.

Most of us could accomplish little without the support of our close friends and families.

For editorial comment from one without local roots, my thanks to Roberta Lewin with whom I worked as script writer while preparing for the production of a historical film, "It Happened Here," produced by New Jersey Public Television. Our youngest grand-daughter, Abigail Hope, a high school junior, gave a thorough critique. Rev. Merry Hope Meloy provided editing help with early chapters, and Dick, my husband, rescued me from numerous computer tangles and endured boring dinners. The manuscript could not have been published without the help of Dr. Meg Meloy who handled manuscript preparation, formatting, and found a publisher. She opened a door when I faced a wall. Finally, my deep appreciation goes to Ted Gilley who edited the final version.

My heartfelt thanks to all!

ALICE McFEELY MELOY

Map of Franklin County, PA

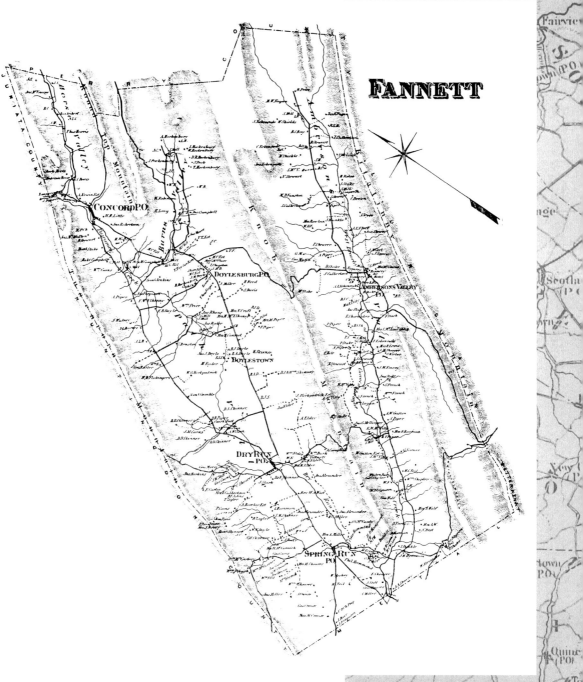

Fannett Township
(Concord to Spring Run)

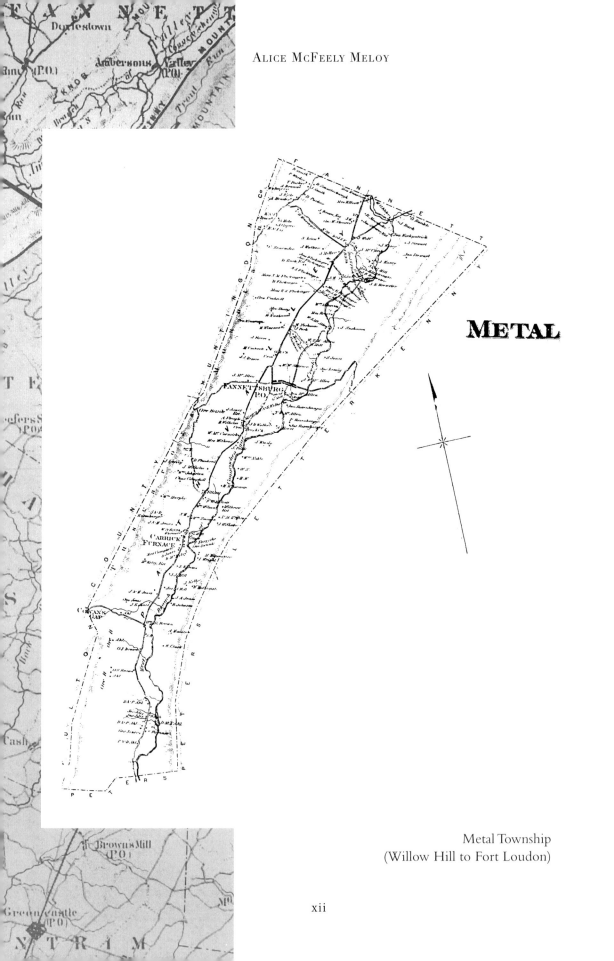

METAL

Metal Township
(Willow Hill to Fort Loudon)

PATH VALLEY AND THE INDIANS

CHAPTER ONE

O N A CLEAR SUMMER NIGHT, under a full moon and meadows lit with dancing fireflies, one can almost hear the sounds of moccasin feet and voices long stilled. This was the home of the Tuscarora Indians who loved this valley. As one Indian said, "Until the new heavens arch themselves and until the new earth comes, our Pennsylvania valleys will lie smiling in the sunlight, our streams will go singing to the sea, and our Pennsylvania mountains will lift their summit to the sky."

Path Valley was named for the Indian path that ran the length of the valley and was used by the Tuscarora tribe when they were forced to leave their home in North Carolina. Eventually, they became part of the Iroquois nation in New York State, but for many long years they lingered in the area. The mountain on the western side of the valley bears their name.

The intrusion of the white settlers around 1734 brought into conflict two very different sets of values. Individual ownership of land was a concept foreign to the Indian. While the Indian "trod lightly through his natural environment, merging himself sympathetically into the world of living and non-living things," the white man came to tame the wilderness and make it home. But, as Chief Seattle of the Duwamish tribe once asked, "What is man without the beasts? If all the beasts were gone, men would die from great loneliness of spirit, for whatever happens to the beasts also happens to man."

Living in tune with nature, the Indians were careful to leave a few kernels of corn or wild beans from their harvest for the field mouse. They never robbed the bee of all its honey. Killing only what was needed and never animals with young, they walked reverently among the trees and streams. Their footprint on the land was light and their joy in life evident. When the first whites entered the woods, they overheard the giggles and chatter of young Indian girls as they combed the woods and meadows for food.

The Tuscarora Indians are first mentioned in *The History of Carolina* by John Lawson who described the Tuscarora's as among the most advanced of many tribes, saying they were "amiable, mild and kind, ingenious and industrious." Men and women worked together cultivating large gardens of vegetables. They were generous with their produce, freely sharing food and showing hospitality to those who visited their villages. Sadly, Larson adds, "They are really better to us than we have been to them...We allow them to walk by our doors hungry."

In 1710, the Tuscarora's had a population of 6,000 and lived in fifteen towns in North Carolina, but that was to change. The whites took their land at will without paying a purchase price. Worse yet, whites captured and sold Tuscarora Indians into slavery. Some were sent as far away as the West Indies. A brisk slave trade was carried on up and down the coast. Even Pennsylvania, known for having an amiable relationship with the Indians, was involved.

Meanwhile, the Tuscarora's were being decimated by the effects of rum, smallpox, and other diseases, all brought into their lives by white men. Some estimate that in the end only one sixth of their original population survived. Nevertheless, as late as 1737, observers of culture declared that the Tuscarora's were among the most civilized tribes who lived along the Eastern Seaboard.

Peace-loving, the Tuscarora's wished to avoid war with the whites, so they petitioned the government of Pennsylvania in 1710. They requested a home and to be friends among Christian people, the ability to fetch wood and water in safety, and security for their children to play without fear. Young men petitioned for the privilege of leaving their towns to search for meat without fear of death or slavery. The entire tribe asked for peace and an end to their enslavement and murder, so they would not live in fear of "a mouse or anything that ruffles the leaves." Finally, they asked for an "official path or means of communication between them." Unfortunately, their petition was not granted, but in 1713 they began moving northward and ultimately became the sixth nation of the Iroquois Confederation.

The Iroquois Confederacy was well organized with each tribe keeping its own identity. Once a year, runners were sent to summon the chiefs to meet as representatives to the council. Each tribe participated and together they attempted to bring harmony out of differences. They never debated a problem when it was first brought up, but gave each tribe a chance to reach consensus among its own group. When that was accomplished, they presented their unified view to the other tribes.

Democratic in spirit, the Iroquois Confederacy believed the Great Spirit had chosen them to lead all men into a lasting peace. They envisioned a worldwide league of tribes or nations living in a land where one could go anywhere without fear. The Tree of Peace was represented by a great white pine "rising to meet the sun." In time, the white race would find they had much to learn from their neighbors.

The Tuscarora move north occurred in stages over many years; some estimate ninety. Some Tuscarora's stopped and settled in Path Valley finding good hunting and streams filled with fish. Indian arrowheads have been found in fields, along creeks, and around the pond in Spring Run, lasting reminders of the first people to call Path Valley home.

Meanwhile, white settlers from the eastern part of Pennsylvania were edging farther and farther west. Some found their way into Path Valley. For the most part, they were Scots who came by way of Ireland. Others came directly from Scotland remembering massive stone castles bearing their clan's name, and the grandeur of Scotland's lonely mountains and sparkling lochs.

Those who came by way of Ireland had endured much. Early in the 18th century, James I opened a plantation in Ulster and encouraged English and Scots to settle there. Many Lowland Scots crossed the Irish Sea seeking to improve their economic position. In Ulster, the Scots transformed a land of marshes and mud cabins into a land of towns and villages where trade was established. Churches and schools dotted the landscape.

The Scots' high hopes for a future in Ireland soon turned to dismal disappointment. Economic reversals eroded their growing prosperity. In 1717, land leased to them by the English was renewable at double or triple the original fee. After turning desolate ground into a prosperous farming district, the Scots were now penalized with such increased rents that farming became unprofitable.

Furthermore, a new ruling limited the exportation of wool to any market outside England and Wales. This was a tremendous blow to the woolen industry which formed the foundation of the region's prosperity. A series of poor crops followed and many families faced starvation. The final blow was the decline of linen manufacturing after 1770.

The Scots also faced religious persecution after the Church of England was declared the official religion. For the most part, Scots were Presbyterian. Marriages performed by Presbyterian clergy were not deemed legal and fines were imposed. Presbyterian ministers' right to conduct graveside services for their own members was questioned. Presbyterian churches could no longer be erected on estates belonging to Episcopal landlords. Furthermore, Presbyterians were forced to pay tithes to support clergy in the Church of England and excluded from holding civil or military offices unless they consented to take Communion in the established Church.

In response, many Scots began making plans to migrate to America. Money was stashed away in stockings and hidden purses. Others with large families became indentured servants to pay for their passage. The Scots undertook terrifying odds as they crowded onto ships often unfit for trans-Atlantic voyages. Even under the best of circumstances, the trip was dangerous. Captains and crews were sometimes unacquainted with winds and currents. Blown off course, some ships took five months or more to cross the Atlantic. Starvation took its toll on passengers. Overcrowding created rampant disease. Still, the Scots loaded their gear, said their final goodbyes, and faced the open seas with resolve and hope. Their destiny was America in general, Pennsylvania in particular.

Too late, the English became aware that Ireland was quickly losing its prominent and useful Scottish inhabitants. The English proprietors urged the Synod of the Presbyterian Church to use its influence and compel its members to stay, but the exodus continued.

In America, the arrival of the Scots-Irish was viewed with some alarm by the Quakers in Philadelphia. Between 1771 and 1773, 101 ships sailed from Ulster ports. Approximately 32,000 Scots-Irish landed in Philadelphia or in Newcastle and Lewes, Delaware. Secretary Logan of Pennsylvania wrote, "It looks as if Ireland is to send all its inhabitants." Many were destined to live on the frontier of Pennsylvania where the terrain more closely resembled the land of Scotland. They left problems behind, but there were challenges ahead.

The new immigrants pushed westward seeking land. Pennsylvania had set the boundary for new settlements at the Susquehanna River, but the hunger for a home motivated many to push beyond that point. Some families crossed the mountains into Path Valley and Juniata Valley. According to records, Thomas Doyle and Samuel Bechtel were settled in Path Valley by 1737. Thomas Doyle bought his land from the Indians, or thought he had. On some old maps, the northern part of Path Valley appeared to be part of Hopewell Township, Lancaster County, incorrectly indicating it was open for settlement. Traders had already arrived and the Pyatt trading post established near Dry Run. Unfortunately, the Pennsylvania government had not yet officially purchased the land from the Iroquois Confederation.

In these early days, relations between the Indians and whites were, for the most part, friendly. During William Penn's administration, there had been no Indian warfare in Pennsylvania. In Path Valley, it was reported that Indians helped white families with food in winter, and at times white children were left in their care. According to correspondence from Fort

Duquesne, the Tuscarora Indians played an important role in protecting whites along the frontier.

A German Reformed minister, Michael Schlatter, had an exalted opinion of the Indians. He believed them to be hospitable and wrote, "As late as 1748, there were many Indians within Franklin County, well disposed and very obliging and not disinclined towards Christians when not made drunk."

The relationship between most whites and Indians continued to be amiable and helpful until the beauty and fertility of Path Valley attracted a swiftly growing stream of settlers. Finally, the Indians became alarmed. Path Valley was one of their favorite hunting grounds. Deer and rabbits were plentiful and the creeks were filled with fish.

In the summer of 1741, the sheriff and three magistrates were sent to Path Valley to "turn off the people there settled." However, some Indians said they were content and things should be left as they were until the Six Nation chiefs could come and converse with the governor of Pennsylvania. It appeared there was no consensus of opinion about the presence of the whites among the Indians themselves at this point. Not all Indians were alike and neither were all whites. Some were honest and fair, holding out the hand of friendship. Other Indians noted the arrogance and disdain of certain whites.

Conrad Weiser served as an interpreter and diplomat in councils between the Pennsylvania Colony and the Indians. He was invaluable in his work to prevent bloodshed and keep peace between Indian tribes and the new settlers. On August 11, 1748, Weiser made a trip to Black Log on one of many missions. He was accompanied by George Croghan and William Franklin. In all likelihood, their route took them over the mountain path between Amberson and Doylesburg and through the gap at Concord.

In 1744, complaints from Indians reached colonial authorities. Magistrates were called in to deal with the situation. Warnings from government officials were posted on July 1, 1749 in Juniata Valley and Path Valley, telling settlers to move eastward by November 1, 1749. Few heeded the warning. It was not until 1750 that action took place.

In May, a conference with whites and Indians was held at George Croghan's residence in Pennsboro Township, Cumberland County. Five

Indians, three from Shamokin, two of whom were sons of the late Shikellamy, attended. They were assured that the whites west of the Susquehanna River would be removed.

On May 30th, 1750, a company of magistrates and Indians on horseback set out for Path Valley. Richard Peter, secretary to the governor, Benjamin Chambers, William Maxwell, William Allison, John Findlay, and others were part of the contingency. Some sources include the names of Conrad Weiser, Andrew Montour, a Mohawk chief, and an interpreter.

One can imagine the procession of officials riding through lush green forests dotted with May apples, dogtooth violets, and spring beauties in natural meadows. Everything was bursting with new life, but for the settlers, the arrival of the officials meant the end of a dream. They were being evicted!

The group came to one cabin and then another, commanding the settlers to remove their possessions. Abraham Slack's cabin was torched and went up in flames, then James Blair's. Dark columns of smoke rose from the forest giving warning to other inhabitants of the valley. Before the day was over, the cabins belonging to Moses Moore, Arthur Dunlop, Alexander McCartie, David Lewis, Adam McCartie, Felix Doyle, Reynold Alexander, Samuel Patterson, Robert Baker, John Armstrong, John Potts, Andrew Dunlop, Robert Wilson, Jacob Pyatt, and William Ramage were reduced to smoldering timbers and ashes.

The officials told the settlers they were charged with trespassing, bound in recognizance of 100 pounds and required to appear on the first day the Cumberland County Court was held in Shippensburg. It was a heartbreaking beginning to their new life in Pennsylvania.

Years later, J. M. Pomeroy wrote in the Franklin Repository (1874), that these settlers "executed the bonds...and very cheerfully and voluntarily took everything out of the log houses and assisted in burning them." Undoubtedly, there were tears as children watched the only home they knew consigned to flames. Items from their homes were loaded on their backs and the backs of pack horses. The next question was where to go. Fortunately, those who carried out the orders were sympathetic and kind. Families who could not raise the hundred pounds were given aid, and all were told they could resettle on any part of the two million acres east of the Susquehanna River that had been recently purchased from the Indians.

For the next week, embers of the cabins smoked and smoldered in the night air. Soon weeds flourished in the small gardens that had been planted and the woods for the moment were almost silent. One report of the event noted, "It may be proper to add that the... log houses which were burned were of no considerable value being of such as country people erect in a day or two and cost only the charge of an entertainment." While this analysis of value may have been correct, the cabins were home to those who lived there. As families plodded down paths leading to Shippensburg and Carlisle, they faced the fact that their dream had gone up in smoke, but they continued to hold fast to hope.

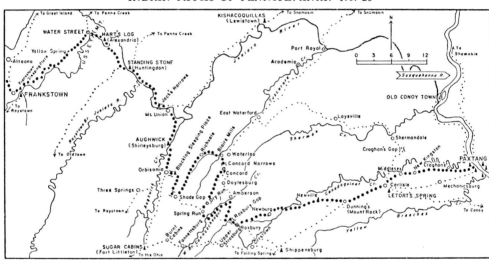

INDIAN PATHS OF PENNSYLVANIA: No. 26

FRANKSTOWN PATH, EAST

Indian paths,
including the Tuscarora Path

THE SCOTS
ARE COMING TO STAY

CHAPTER TWO

*B*ENJAMIN FRANKLIN SQUIRMED in his hard chair and wiped his brow. The June heat in Albany, New York was oppressive, and his body still ached from the rigors of travel. Days had passed at the 1754 Albany Conference where leaders of the Iroquois nations and representatives of the provincial government of Pennsylvania had convened for negotiations. Longingly, Ben Franklin thought of the comforts of his home near the Delaware River and of the pleasures he had forsaken in Philadelphia. He nodded sympathetically to his fellow assemblymen, Isaac Norris, John Penn, and Richard Peters. All of them rather envied Pennsylvania Governor Hamilton's inability to be present.

The business at hand was important, however. With each shipload of new colonists, the pressure to settle in areas west of the Susquehanna River increased. Complaints had been growing about white settlers trespassing on

Indian land. One of the goals of the Pennsylvanians was to acquire new land for settlement.

On July 6, 1754, the chiefs of the Six Iroquois Nations signed a deed that conveyed to Pennsylvania "all the land extending on the west side of the Susquehanna River from the Blue Mountains to a mile above the mouth of the Kayarondihagh (Penn's Creek); thence along the western boundary to the Blue Mountains; and thence along the Blue Mountains to the place of beginning."

The Delawares and Shawnees, already suffering from an invasion of white settlers in the eastern part of the province, were enraged. They had been steadily forced westward. Now the Iroquois nation had sold some of their favorite hunting ground without consulting them. The transaction would lead to problems in the future.

When the land office opened on February 3, 1755, settlers coming from Scotland, Ireland, and Eastern Pennsylvania hurried to apply warrants. Snow still swirled in the mountains and icy winds moaned in the trees. Jacob Pyatt's trading post near Dry Run was already in operation. In 1756, Richard and John Coulter purchased a large body of land in the upper end of the valley. Francis Amberson made an "improvement" in Amberson Valley in 1763. Barnabas Clark, from whom "Clark's Knob" received its name, arrived. Meanwhile, John Ward, Felix Doyle, Cromwell McVitty, John Blair's heirs, John Elliott, John Sands, Alexander Lowery and a host of others made their way to Path Valley to build cabins and make a home.

Tuscarora, Delaware, and Shawnee Indians lingered in the area for a number of years. Burns Valley, in particular, continued to be their home. Cape Horn Road in the Concord Narrows was named for an Indian chief who wore a cape trimmed with rattles from a rattlesnake. At one time, there was an Indian village near the Tuscarora creek. Deep friendships continued between whites and Indians until the Revolutionary War period.

In the background however, two major world powers, Britain and France, were fighting to extend their power and acquire territory in the new world. Eventually, the struggle would involve Indian tribes and affect the safety of those living in Path Valley.

The French claimed the land beyond the Appalachian Mountains and had explored many areas completely unknown to the British who had settled along the coastline. French exploration of rivers had taken them as far north as Canada and south to the mouth of the Mississippi giving them a broad knowledge of the new world. They came as explorers, traders, and speculators, and often had closer ties with the Indians than the British.

As Walter O'Meara described the situation, "French soldiers, traders, and even officers married Indian women, raised families of half-breed children, dressed, talked, acted, and finally thought as Indians." Unlike the British, the French were not intent on turning Indian hunting grounds into farms and towns driving away the game on which the Indians depended. They came as traders.

The British, on the other hand, exhibited little understanding of Indian nature and dignity. Often arrogant, sometimes grasping, they ignored tribal rights. Although they did little to make the Indians love them, they offered better guns and blankets at lower prices than the French, and there was never a shortage of rum. Wooed by both French and British, the Indians played both sides in the struggle.

On May of 1755, the British took action sending Major-General Sir Edward Braddock to take Fort Duquesne, located in what is now Pittsburgh. Well prepared with artillery and equipment, Braddock commanded some 1,350 well trained British troops and 500 colonials. As his troops marched west in formation, Braddock was not prepared for the morale-shattering shrieks of a completely invisible Indian enemy hidden among trees in the steep terrain. Americans broke ranks and fought Indian style, learning an invaluable lesson for the future. The British troops suffered tremendous losses. General Braddock was killed! The French controlled western Pennsylvania and the Scots-Irish on the Pennsylvania frontier would bear the brunt of the conflict leading to the French and Indian War which officially began in 1756 and ended in 1763.

On October 31, 1755, the Shawnee and Delaware Indians attacked the area around Little Cove near Mercersburg. Many people were killed. A letter written from Shippensburg on November 2, 1755 described the situation.

Dear and Honored Sir;

We are in great confusion here at present. We received express last night that the Indians and French are in a large body in the cove, a little way from William Maxwell, Esq., and that they immediately intend to fall down upon this country. We, for the past two days, have been working at our Fort here, and believe shall work this day Sunday. This town is full of people, they being all moving in with their families - five and six families in a house. We are in great want of arms and ammunition; but with what we have we are determined to give the enemy a war reception as we can. Some of our people have been taken prisoners by this party, and have made their escape from them, and came to us this morning.

As our Fort goes on here with great vigor, and expect it to be finished in 15 days, in which we intend to place all the women and children; it would be greatly encouraging could we have reason to expect assistance from Philadelphia by private donation of Swivels, a few great guns, small arms and ammunition, we would send our own wagons for them; and we do not doubt that upon proper application that something of this kind will be done for us from Philadelphia. We have 100 men working at Fort Morris with heart and hand every day.

James Burd

A letter from Adam Hoops written from Conococheague on November 6, 1755, tells more about the events in Path Valley.

May it please your Honor:

I have enclosed two qualifications, one of which is Patrick Burns, the bearer, and a tomahawk which was found sticking in the breast of one David McClellan.

The people of Path Valley are all gathered in a small fort, and according to last account are safe. The Great Cove and Conolloways are all burned to ashes, and about 50 persons killed or taken. Numbers of the inhabitants of this county have moved their families, some to York County, and some to Maryland.

Hance Hamilton, Esq., is now at John McDowell's mill with upwards of two hundred men from York County and two hundred from this county... Tomorrow we intend to go to the Cove and Path Valley, in order to bring what cattle and horses the Indians let live. We are informed by a Delaware Indian, who lives amongst us, that on the same day the murder was committed, he saw four hundred Indians in the Cove; and we have reason to believe they are there yet.

The people of Sherman's Creek and Juniata have all come away and left their horses; and there are now about thirty miles of this county laid waste. I'm afraid there will soon be more.

Adam Hoops

With Indians swarming through the woods and over the trails, life for those in Path Valley had become precarious. Crops rotted. Animals, if not taken, were sometimes destroyed. Finally, four hundred militia were sent into Path Valley to bring out what cattle and horses the Indians had left alive.

There were a number of official forts in the county. These were supposed to be manned by twenty-five to seventy-five paid men. Fort Chambers, located at Falling Spring, was a two story house with small windows and a lead roof, surrounded by a stockade. Fort Lowther was built in Carlisle and Fort Morris in Shippensburg. Lyttleton and Shirley also boasted forts. Fort Loudon located at the foot of Path Valley proved very important to inhabitants. Fort Elliott, built in 1754, was located in the middle of the valley at Springtown. Only ten to twelve soldiers were on duty at times, however.

In his book on *Pennsylvania Forts*, Hale Sipes defines a fort as "a strong place of defense and refuge, stockaded and embracing cabins. A station was a parallelogram of cabins, united by palisades to present a wall. A blockhouse, on the other hand, was a strong square, two storied structure, with the upper floor projecting over the lower two feet so inhabitants could fire upon Indians attempting to burn the building." It is surmised that Fort Elliott was of this construction. Other private forts were simply log structures with holes through which pioneers could fire upon the enemy.

There were a number of private forts of this nature throughout Path Valley. Some people say there was a fort near the Round Top north of Doylesburg, but information is scanty. Baker's Fort was probably located near the present stone quarry in Dry Run. Felix, Barnabas, and William Doyle erected a sturdy two story log house at Doylestown and fitted it for warfare. Although they could not afford a lead roof resistant to fire, it was spacious and could accommodate the neighbors. During times of danger, settlers worked at their homesteads, muskets close at hand. As night fell, they gathered at the fort for greater security.

A story about Barnabas Doyle and his wife has been passed down through generations. One evening, they closed the door to their cabin and retreated to the safety of the Doylestown fort. Later that night, Mrs. Doyle suddenly remembered she had left a candle burning in their cabin. Fearing the cabin might catch fire, she started through the dark woods, stumbling over tree roots, listening to the cries of wild animals, wondering if Indians were in the vicinity. She finally reached the cabin, extinguished the candle, and made the long trip back to the fort. Such was the courage of these early settlers.

There might be forts, but arms and ammunition continued to be in short supply. Pleas for weapons and ammunition were, for the most part, ignored. Impatient with the slow response of the Pennsylvania Assembly in Philadelphia to the crisis on the frontier, a group of men loaded dead bodies on a wagon, casualties of Indian attacks, and headed for the city. This protest was a wake-up call.

Eventually, the tide began to turn in favor of the British. Brigadier-General John Forbes with an army of almost 8,000 men forced the French to evacuate Fort Duquesne on November 25, 1758. On his way west, Forbes spent some time at Fort Loudon. Path Valley residents must have looked on in wonder as he and his army passed through the valley. Forbes was an invalid and was carried on a horse litter tied securely by a rope his soldiers held. Indians were told Forbes was so fierce and terrible he had to be restrained until released for battle. A year later, Forbes died in Philadelphia. With the capture of Quebec in 1759 some measure of relief came to the colonists on the frontier.

Although the seven-year French and Indian War did not come to an end until 1763, settlers continued to find their way into Path Valley. In 1760, the Walker brothers, James and Samuel, staked out their claim in lower Path Valley and built a cabin. The family was soon augmented by their parents, Alexander and Mary, and brothers, John, David and Robert. Around the same time, the Elliott brothers, Archibald and Francis, bought land from a squatter. The relative peace was shattered by Pontiac's Rebellion which began in 1763 and lasted until November 1764. Again atrocities occurred and people fled to Fort Loudon.

On the other hand, a number of people north of Path Valley were saved by the act of one Indian to whom Ralph Sterrit had given food and tobacco. One night, the Indian crept to the gate of Bingham's fort in the Tuscarora Valley and whispered to the guard, "Indians plenty as pigeons in the woods." Warned, the settlers at the fort packed up and fled for safety in Cumberland Valley. Eighty persons were saved by one Indian's humane act.

Settlers continued to buy land with a hopeful eye on the future. They learned to have some stand guard while others planted or harvested. Women handled firearms and weapons. Children were taught to watch and listen for unexpected footsteps or an unexplained noise.

The story of the Hayes family is a good example of what life was like on the Pennsylvania frontier. They lived near the Tuscarora Path north of Path Valley. For the sake of safety, a big bell had been placed on top of the house with a rope pulled down through the roof. Mr. Hayes was clearing ground while Mrs. Hayes was cooking in the cabin. The skin had been removed from the cabin window for ventilation. Mrs. Hayes looked up to see an Indian coming in through the opening. Instinctively, she scooped up coals from the fireplace and threw them on the intruder who fled screaming in pain. Quickly she rang the bell and gave the alarm. One of the children pointed out two Indians under an apple tree and two near the barn. Another was ready to climb down the chimney. Mrs. Hayes threw goose feathers she had been saving into the fire which sent such smoke rolling up the chimney, the Indian was smothered and fell into the fireplace. Mr. Hayes ran through the door, and quickly loaded his musket. He shot the two Indians under the apple tree. A child yelled, "Pappie, there are two out by the barn!" Shooting toward the barn, he managed to dispatch the enemy. Cleanup followed. One charred body remained in the fireplace. Mrs. Hayes and the children sat in the woodshed until the burnt corpse was removed. Mrs. Hayes said, "I refuse to cook in that fireplace until it is thoroughly cleaned and limed!" Such was life on the frontier.

Although only one person was killed by Indians in Path Valley, others were captured. A little red-headed girl was kidnapped near what is now Doylesburg. According to family tradition, she was playing near their log cabin when a group of Indians passed by. Her mother came to the door in time to see the curly-haired little girl smiling at her over the shoulder of an Indian who was carrying her away. The mother ran for an old tin horn and blew with all her might. The neighbors came running, but the little girl had disappeared forever. Years later, leaders reported seeing a red-haired squaw much farther west beyond the mountains. The girl's name was Susan Taylor. According to Bob Crouse, each subsequent generation of that family, named a daughter Susan in memory of the little girl who was taken so long ago.

Other families also preserved memories of those early days. Captain J. H. Walker shared the following story about an ancestor who lived near Fannettsburg. In August 1762, James Walker was captured by Indians while returning from Fort Loudon. The Indians fired on him, killing his horse. As he tried to escape, Walker's baggy pantaloons got caught in the brush, and he was captured. His saddle was placed on his back, and he was forced to climb the Tuscarora Mountain to the west. When they came to Fort Littleton, Walker's hopes rose. Horses were grazing around the fort which surely meant there were soldiers scouting in the area. That night he was tied and guarded by two Indians who slept on either side of him.

The next day, the Indians attempted to steal the horses. They were unsuccessful and assigned the task to Walker. Fastening a rope of hickory bark to Walker's leg while they held the other end, they sent him on his mission. He feigned real effort, but he was not anxious to obtain a mount and ride farther west, increasing the mileage from home. Fort Littleton was filled with activity and for a day the Indians sat watching. Walker was frustrated. Help was near, but he knew he would be killed in seconds if he gave away their position. Finally, the group continued on.

After crossing the Raystown branch of the Juniata River, they approached an Indian settlement. The party divided, and Walker was left with two Indians who tied him up for the night and fell into a sound sleep. Walker snored loudly, watching the scene between the fringes of his eyelashes. He quietly struggled with the ropes that tied his hands, careful lest his movement wake the Indians. The knife secreted in his belt was hard to reach. Finally, he got one hand loose and worked the knife out of its hiding place. Just as he cut the cords, one of the Indians startled and sat up. He checked the prisoner who was snoring and the fire which had ebbed, and then went back to sleep. The time had come. As Walker got to his feet, the same Indian woke and grabbed his tomahawk. In desperation, Walker grasped him by the hair and thrust his knife into his throat. The commotion awakened the other Indian. Fortunately, he fled. For the moment, Walker was free.

He fled eastward, trying to put as much space between him and the dead Indian as possible. He knew a war party would soon be searching the woods for him. The main Indian trail was too dangerous to use so he had to cut through the brush. He traveled at night, and hid during the day. Stumbling over rocks, fearful of rattlesnakes and packs of wolves, he at times became confused and wandered toward the west, only to correct him after hours of tortuous walking. He walked through rain and lightning storms so violent the very mountains seemed about to explode. Gnawing hunger was his constant companion. Berries and roots kept him alive. Finally, he stumbled into Fort Lyttleton more dead than alive. It took days of recuperation before he was strong enough to continue home.

Less than a year later, on March 22, 1763, Indians set fire to the Walker barn owned by James and Samuel and located a mile south of Fannettsburg. The Walkers managed to save six horses. Unfortunately, the horses ran to the creek where the Indians amused themselves by shooting them. Only one horse survived. Seeing flames, neighbors gathered. Meanwhile, the Indians quietly stole away in the darkness and escaped over the mountain. "Those pesky Indians," the settlers raged in disgust. Members of the Walker family still have in their possession some of the scorched wheat that survived the fire.

In spite of the uncertainties of pioneer life, more settlers arrived. The Scots-Irish and the Germans who began to join them were undeterred. These early families continued to clear ground, fell trees, and build homes. They were here to stay.

Site of Elliott's Fort,
built in 1754, at Springtown

Springhouse at Elliott's Fort
in Springtown

HOME SWEET HOME

CHAPTER THREE

*P*EOPLE CONTINUED TO ARRIVE in Path Valley and build their cabins in spite of numerous hardships and dangers. The Appalachian Mountains reminded many Scots-Irish of the mountains and rolling hills of Scotland. Later, Germans who found land scarce farther east came to join them.

Families came on foot with their worldly possessions either loaded on their backs or on a pack horse. Often the father led the procession carrying an axe and a musket on his shoulders. The mother followed, bearing either an infant lulled to sleep by constant motion or food to sustain them on their journey. Each child followed bearing a bundle or sometimes parts to a spinning wheel. A Bible and a hornbook (alphabet book) were usually among their meager belongings. The more affluent owned more than one pack horse and could bring some of the amenities of civilization into the wilderness. The stream of newcomers, mostly Presbyterians, was steady, interrupted only by the severe storms of winter.

In one case, even an icy deep snow failed to deter the arrival of new set-tlers to the area. Alexander McElroy and his family were attempting to climb the slippery crust of snow on the eastern side of the Tuscarora Mountain. When they got to the top, inspiration struck. Mr. McElroy tied their feather bed into a convenient bundle, took his youngest child in his arms, mounted his improvised sled and said to his wife, "Give me a push." Away he flew down the Tuscarora Mountain, reaching his destination safely. Mrs. McElroy and several younger children followed in his wake, using pillows as sleds. Slipping and sliding, the horse followed as best he could.

Pioneers chose their land carefully. Having a source of water, either spring or stream, close at hand was a priority. Drainage was also important. Ever aware of the seasons, they often built their dwellings with a southern exposure to catch the warming rays of the sun during the winter months. Others built their homes into banks for protection against the westerly winter winds.

Above all, these early pioneers had a deep relationship with the soil. They obtained a fairly accurate sense of its fertility by rubbing the soil between their fingers, looking at its coloration and feeling its texture. Many tasted the soil, describing acid soil as fizzy and crackly with a bite. Neutral soil had the odor and taste of humus, whereas alkaline soil tasted chalky and coated the tongue. Later, they would acquire manure and lime to correct some soil conditions, but these early settlers were well aware that their lives and welfare depended on their relationship with the soil and nature's gifts of sun and rain.

The dwellings were small by our standards, rarely larger than 18x24 feet. This size structure was home to two parents and in most cases, a brood of children. The chimney dominated the cabin on the exterior, the fireplace the interior. It was a constant and backbreaking job to keep the fire burning which not only provided heat but light and fuel to cook their food. The back log, sometimes six feet long, often required the strength of several men to roll into place. The sound of the axe constantly echoed through the woods as family members worked to replenish the wood supply.

The fireplace was the center of family life although an imperfect source of heat. One person said, "You froze on one side and were parched on the other." Children often sat on a narrow stone seat built into one end of some fireplaces. From there, they could watch the endless activity in the cabin until called into service. At night, they could look up through the chimney and see the stars glittering in the darkness. Around the fire, parents taught their children to read using the hornbook and Bible.

The forest not only provided fuel for the fire, logs for the cabin, lumber for furniture, and material for utensils, but a habitat for wild animals and fowl that provided food for the table and skins for clothing. In the dark recesses of the woods, wolves and coyotes howled and birds and squirrels chattered. While the forest gave gifts, it also had to be tamed and cleared to yield fields and pastures.

Work began in the early morning. Mattresses made of corn-husk tick or straw rustled as parents emerged from blankets, made of wool or animal skins, to brave the cold air. The cabin was dark with the exception of the smoldering fire and the faint light of dawn. Some cabins boasted a window covered with oilskin. Others had little more than a slit between two logs.

Shivering in the dim light the mother dressed, wrapped herself in her shawl, and stirred the embers of fire back to life. The father dressed in a deerskin hunting shirt that reached to his knees and was belted in with enough overlap to provide space for carrying anything from tools to food.

When the fire had started to blaze, the children dashed to the hearth from trundle beds that had been pulled out from beneath their parents' bedstead, a crude affair made of small logs with one end fastened to the wall of the cabin and the other supported on crossed sticks. The earthen floor was cold!

Keeping the fire going was important. If the fire died during the night, it meant a two or three mile walk to get coals from a neighbor and a long wait before a new fire could be laid and relief found from the penetrating cold. Some were clever enough to create sparks through friction, but it required very dry wood or kindling. However, in most cases flames soon darted high in the fireplace, and the heat began to penetrate the clinging cold and provide light for the morning activity.

Cooking breakfast was no simple matter. The utensils were heavy. Some families owned only a stewing pot which held five to ten gallons and weighed twenty pounds or more. Before iron cranes were available, these pots were supported by a hickory crane that sometimes weakened through constant charring, spilling the contents of hot stew or mush on the cook. Women, often pregnant, lifted these heavy kettles on and off the fire, sometimes burning their faces and blistering their hands. The more affluent owned not only a stewing pot, but a long handled frying pan, a three-legged short-handled spider, and an oven with feet and a fitted lid.

Corn was the staff of life in central Pennsylvania and was served in a variety of ways. Cornpone, a type of bread, was often served for breakfast and lunch followed by mush and milk or mush and molasses for supper. The diet changed to a tasty stew if some member of the family was fortunate enough to kill a deer, rabbit or squirrel often called "mountain meat."

Cornpone or not, when everyone was ready for breakfast, they seated themselves at a table made either of split logs with poles for legs or rough boards laid on supports similar to saw horses. Three-legged stools sufficed for seats. The dishes were often carved wooden trenchers, but many families simply deposited the stewing kettle in the middle of the table and with spoons carved from laurel, each person ate from the common pot. Gourds were used for cups, bowls, and dippers. Forks were unknown. Knives were used not only to cut food but to convey it to the mouth. When peas became plentiful, someone penned these lines, "I eat my peas with honey; I've done it all my life. It makes the peas taste funny; but it keeps them on my knife." More prosperous families sometimes had treasured pewter plates and tankards from the old country. These were brought forth to celebrate special occasions.

When breakfast was over, there were chores for the entire family. An older child looked after the toddler or baby in a cradle by the fireplace. Stronger children were sent to the spring or creek for water. Others kept the fire supplied with wood. The eldest girl might be set to work grinding corn into meal with mortar and pestle.

The whirl of the spinning wheel and the clack of the loom were music in a pioneer cabin, and were often accompanied by members of the family humming or singing a song or psalm. The women made all the clothing through a long process of planting and harvesting flax, processing it, spinning, weaving, cutting and sewing by hand. After sheep came to the frontier, there was linsey-woolsey, a material used for much of the clothing, and woven of flax and wool. It was a stiff, hardy, sometimes scratchy material. One black sheep was kept to provide wool for stockings and gray and black clothing. Some ambitious women dyed material by using plants and berries from the woods and fields. Men tanned skins for leather products like shoes and other types of attire.

As time passed, the family unit became more productive, and "best clothes" were bought and displayed on wooden pegs driven into the cabin walls. In one instance, a blue broadcloth coat bought by the men in one family was worn by fifteen or more grooms on their wedding day. Fancy Sunday-going-to-meeting clothes earned the wrath of at least one rural clergyman who wrote, "Thus calico and silk, and sin by slow degrees kept coming in." Nevertheless, dress clothing, shoe buckles, and even bonnets were gradually acquired, treasured, and bequeathed to the next generation.

The list of responsibilities allotted to women and their daughters was formidable. Some girls were married by age fourteen or fifteen, so most girls were taught domestic skills from the time they could talk. Women not only combed, carded, spun, knitted and made all the clothing, but raised chickens, took care of livestock, milked cows, dried and preserved food, carried water, cleaned and cooked. Pregnancy was a frequent condition. Many women had a baby every other year.

Feeding a family required planning and frugality. The products of field and forest were gathered and preserved according to the season. There were wild crab apples, elderberries, blackberries, huckleberries, raspberries, goose-berries, wild strawberries, red and yellow plums, and wild onion. After the land was cleared, many families planted apple and peach orchards. Pumpkin rings, peppers, herbs and other plants were hung from the beams of cabins and dried.

Flax seed, mustard, bark of wild cherry, slippery elm, willow, sassafras, and Virginia snake root were collected for medicinal purposes and were part of a list of remedies for fevers and colds.

Substitutes for English tea and coffee were difficult to find. Mint, sas-safras, catnip, raspberry leaves and pennyroyal were dried and brewed into steaming beverages. Sage and thyme were added to the list when gardens were planted. Roasted grains were also brewed as coffee substitutes. When apple orchards finally produced fruit, cider became a staple. Whiskey was prized and strangely enough some people said it could be drunk in copious amounts without causing intoxication.

While the woman of the household found her days filled with incessant labor, the man faced days of toil and danger. Every acre the pioneer acquired had to be defended with rifle and cleared with axe. The farmers used two methods of clearing land. Many landowners girdled the trees which killed them and then farmed around the skeletons. In time, the trees decayed making removal relatively easy. Other farmers grubbed, chopped, and burned until the land was cleared, but that method destroyed the humus and the land lost some of its fertility. Clearing the ground was a major priority. There were hungry mouths to feed!

Farm tools were crude. The earliest harrows were made of thorn bushes, followed by those made in the shape of an "A" with wooden teeth. Improvement brought plows which were nothing more than wooden mold boards with a cutting edge faced with a strip of metal. Seeds were simply thrown, then harrowed in. Corn was planted in hills and cultivated with a hoe. Scythes were used to cut grass; sickles, wheat and rye. A man working from sunrise to sunset could cut from one to two acres a day. Threshing went on all winter. The grain was separated from the chaff with flails and tossed in the air with either pitchfork or winnowing fan. Later, pigs and cows were acquired and roamed the woods until crude barns were built for shelter.

As the sun sank in the west, most families gathered to eat mush and milk. By the light of the fire, females knitted while males made harnesses. Children were taught to read the Bible at an early age and to memorize the Westminster Catechism. Before the fire was banked for the evening, the family listened to a reading from Scripture and prayed together finding strength to conquer difficulties. Meanwhile, they dreamed of a kirk, a church in their midst.

KEEPING THE FAITH

CHAPTER FOUR

Most of Path Valley's early settlers were Scots-Irish Presbyterians. They were people of deep faith, and they remembered their churches in Scotland and Ireland with longing. Some families kept documents that attested to the fact they were members in good standing of a church in the old country. At times, settlers who had served as elders in their home churches in Scotland and Ireland would gather neighbors for worship outdoors in meadows or groves of trees. During inclement weather, the gatherings took place in barns or homes if the buildings were large enough. The infrequency of these gatherings and the lack of pastoral leadership only strengthened the settlers' desire for a kirk and a minister.

According to the minutes of Donegal Presbytery, a Rev. John Beard preached the first sermon in Path Valley on the second Sabbath of April, 1762, "when the war whoop of the Indian still was heard." He also held a week day service near the present site of Waterloo in Juniata County. Other itinerant ministers followed, but not on any regular basis. A Rev. John Hoge visited in 1765. A "rudely constructed platform" was erected near Waterloo as a preaching station.

The Presbyterian Church was concerned about its members who were scattered over the vast frontier. The Corporation for the Relief of the Poor and Distressed, a Presbyterian organization, sent Rev. Charles Beatty abroad to gather funds from home churches in England, Scotland and Ireland. The money was to be used to support people living in precarious conditions on the frontier. In spite of the dangers and time required to travel, colonial Presbyterians maintained close ties to Scotland and Ireland.

Many pastors were educated in Britain or Scotland and then came to the colonies to serve congregations. Even in the wilds of the Pennsylvania frontier, Presbyterians demanded educated ministers. The examinations for licensure and ordination were as rigorous for a minister preaching in a small log church as for a minister serving a church of cathedral proportions in the British Isles.

In August 1766, action was taken at a meeting of the Synods of New York and Philadelphia to send Rev. Charles Beatty, pastor at Neshaminy, and Rev. George Duffield serving in Carlisle, to the frontiers of Pennsylvania to visit Presbyterians and see how they were faring. Rev. Beatty was no stranger to Pennsylvania. Active as minister, missionary, and chaplain, Beatty had been commissioned to serve as chaplain in the First Battalion of Pennsylvania under Colonel Armstrong and General Forbes on June 9, 1758. When the British flag was raised over Fort Duquesne, Rev. Beatty was appointed to preach a Thanksgiving sermon. There is no record of attendance at that service, but Beatty had once complained to Ben Franklin that too few people attended preaching and prayer services. Quick with advice, Franklin said, "It is perhaps, below the dignity of your profession to act as steward of the rum, but if you were to deal it out, and only just after prayers, you would have them all about you." The story goes that Beatty heeded the suggestion, and the numbers grew.

In 1766, Rev. Beatty and Rev. Duffield made a visit to the area. News of their arrival traveled quickly along the Tuscarora Path. "There will be preaching! There will be worship!" Soon, everyone was busy making preparations. Children were sent scampering to the nearest spring to bring water to heat. Strong homemade soap made from lye and fat was plucked out of crocks. Such an occasion as this required fresh clothes and a clean body. Each member of the family took his or her turn in the slowly cooling, quickly darkening water of the big tub. The roughness of the linsey-woolsey towels removed any dirt that remained after the bath. Excitement mounted as best clothes were carefully brought out of trunks. Extra food was prepared while reviewing the Westminster Catechism in case they were quizzed.

According to Beatty's Journal, he and Duffield traveled south, passing through Juniata County to Lack Township where Beatty preached and Duffield "rode to William Grahams eight miles on his way to Path Valley where he intended to preach on the next Sabbath." Church was held near John Blair's on August 24, 1766 and a "considerable large congregation" was there to worship.

Some sources say the rain was so heavy people crowded into a small log house. Everyone's eyes and ears were fixed on the Rev. Beatty. When one woman's gaze wandered, she saw a rattlesnake slithering into the crowded room. She nudged her husband. He also saw the snake. Fearful lest he interrupt the long awaited sermon, he quietly got to his feet and went in search of a weapon. Suddenly, aware of their unwelcome visitor, people jumped to their feet and went running out the door or crowded into the four corners of the room. The rattlesnake was dispatched quickly and worship resumed, but a gasp again interrupted the service when a second snake made its appearance! After going through the ritual a second time, peace returned. The sermon probably went on for another hour or so.

Beatty's description of the people gathered is quite interesting.

> The number of families…is about seventy. The settlement is not much mixed being almost all of one mind, and a people very unanimous among themselves. They have fixed on a place for a meeting house

about eight or nine miles from the head of the valley where they pro-
pose to build a house of square logs fifty feet by twenty-six. The valley
will admit of a number more settlers in it, and they expect to be able
to support a minister after some years, but at present are as the other
valleys just beginning to recover...after their late distresses by the war...
After the sermon I rode home with Francis Elliot and lodged.

Mr. Elliott was known for offering fine accommodations at his small tavern
located near the Fort in Springtown, Path Valley.

Rev. Beatty kept a journal of the trip through central Pennsylvania. In
one entry, he wrote the following.

The house I preached at today was also attacked by the Indians: some
were killed in the house, and others captured. It was truly affecting
to see, almost in every place on the frontier, marks of the ravages of
the cruel and barbarous enemy. Houses and fences burned, household
furniture destroyed, the cattle killed, and horses either killed or carried
off, and to hear the people relate the horrid scenes that were enacted.
Some saw their parents killed and scalped in a barbarous manner, before
their eyes, and themselves captured.

Beatty and Duffield reported to the Synods of New York and Philadelphia
upon their return.

Before Beatty and Duffield's visit, supply preachers from Donegal
Presbytery had come on several occasions to preach, marry, and catechize,
but these services were rare indeed. Children were expected to memorize
the Westminster Catechism as part of their religious education. They were
then tested by a minister. For the most part, Path Valley Presbyterians had to
take their children to Rev. Robert Cooper at Middle Spring, Rev. King at
West Conococheague, or Rev. Craighead at Rocky Spring. The examina-
tion was intense and the trip was long! After families in Path Valley petitioned for pastoral services, Presbytery gave Rev. Cooper of Middle Spring

the task of traveling to Path Valley to catechize children and supervise the election and ordination of elders.

As early as 1765, John Blair, Randall Alexander, David Elder, and James Montgomery had traveled to Philadelphia to request a charter from John Penn. According to oral history, they were also accompanied by Thomas Doyle, a Roman Catholic. In spite of their religious differences, Thomas as both a neighbor and a friend supported them in their endeavor. The details of the trip are buried in lost history, but they accomplished their task and came home with a warrant in hand "for four acres of land joining David Campbell and James Montgomery, including part of the Spring Run, in Fannett Township in the county of Cumberland for a meeting house of religious worship." The date on the warrant is June 21, 1765, although the survey was not made until June 9, 1768.

The location of a church in Path Valley turned out to be problematic. Presbyterians located in the upper end of the valley held a meeting at James Montgomery's house in Spring Run. They took action to build a church on the land acquired through their land warrant. Meanwhile, Noah Abraham, John Clark, and Patrick Davidson expressed their desire to build the church farther down the valley on land donated by Alexander Walker south of Fannettsburg.

At the October meeting in 1769, Presbytery was asked to intervene. According to the record, "Application was made by commissioners from Path Valley for supplies (ministers), and for the Presbytery to endeavor to accommodate some differences, subsisting among them concerning the situation of a meeting house or meeting houses." Presbytery recommended the following. If there were to be two churches, the upper church should be located near the Holliday home at Dry Run, and the lower church near William Harvey's tract at Springtown or no lower in the valley than McIntire's, one mile south of Fannettsburg.

Presbytery appointed Reverends Duffield, Long, King, and Craighead and an equal number of elders to enter into negotiations. Rev. Roan served as moderator when they met at James Montgomery's home in November, 1769. Elders mentioned from the upper end of the valley were, Randall Alexander,

David Elder, John Holliday and John Mairs. Elders from the lower part of the valley were John Cunningham, Robert Walker, Francis Elliott, Samuel Walker and Archibald Elliott.

By 1769, the two factions had already taken matters into their own hands. Upper Path Valley Church had constructed a building on the site of their warrant from Penn in Spring Run. Lower Path Valley Church had begun laying plans for their building in April, 1769 which was completed in 1774. The churches were built of log and erected quickly. Slabs of wood laid on blocks sufficed as benches. There was no means of heating these structures, but members brought heated stones to keep their feet warm. Both churches had easy access to springs providing water for their congregations and horses. These early church members were rugged and committed to their faith.

In May 17, 1775 minutes of the Synod of New York and Philadelphia record Philip Fithian, native of New Jersey, had been ordained. He was immediately sent on a tour through West Virginia and Pennsylvania during 1775-1776 to report on the needs and conditions of the frontier. Described as "one of the great minds of that era," Fithian had an interesting background. A native of Greenwich, New Jersey, he graduated from the College of New Jersey in Princeton in 1770. He then studied theology under the supervision of Rev. Green and Rev. Hunter. Five ministers met with Fithian to examine his knowledge of both Bible and theology. On December 18, 1774, he preached his first sermon at Deerfield, New Jersey. Interesting to note is the fact that Fithian and a group of "Indians" (other young men) were part of the celebrated New Jersey Tea Party.

During his tour to check on frontier churches, Rev. Fithian had a far reaching preaching schedule that included churches in Path Valley, Cedar Springs, Warrior's Mark, Fort Shirley, Northumberland, and Big Valley. Fithian's journal contains vivid descriptions of life around the time of the American Revolution. In one entry, he reported, "At eleven, left Presbytery and rode to Mr. King's within a mile of Fort Loudon; Mr. Keith along. We rode north into Path Valley." Fithian lodged at Mr. Elliot's noting, "He keeps a genteel house with good accommodations. I saw a young woman, a daughter of his, who has never been over the South Mountain, as elegant in her manner and neat in her dress as most in the city."

On Friday, June 23, he wrote to his sweetheart in Greenwich,

> Passed by the narrows into Tuscarora Valley, a most stony valley; two high mountains on every side. The passage is so narrow, that you may take one stone in your right hand and another in your left and throw each upon a mountain, and they are so high that they obscure more than half the horizon. A rainy dripping day, most uncomfortable for riding among leaves. On the way all day, usually a small path and covered with sharp stones. Arrived about five in the evening, although be soaked, at one James Gray's in a little hamlet in the woods. (Spruce Hill, Juniata Valley) He was kind and received me civilly. Forgive me, my country! I supped on tea! It relieved me, however, and I went to bed soon. He had a good pasture for my horse, and his good wife prepared me a warm and suitable supper. Distance rode today, 28 miles...Expenses at small tavern, one shilling.

His journey continued the next day. He wrote,

> Before breakfast came a Scotch matron with her rock and spindle, twisting away at the flax. I rode on after breakfast to Mr. Samuel Lyon's twelve miles yet in Tuscarora. He lives neat, has glass windows, and apparently a good farm...I rode to the Juniata three miles and stopped just on the other side, at John Harris' Esq. He lives elegantly; in the parlor where I am sitting are three windows, each with 24 lights of glass.

When Fithian got to the Seven Mountains, he warned fellow travelers to be armed with "patience and perseverance...If they are furious and hasty, they may, like the Israelites of long ago, commit sin...and swear."

Fithian had little trust of Indians who appeared plentiful. At times he had trouble finding his way. He said only after "encountering several men who smelled strongly of whiskey one dark night, could he be assured that he was on the path leading to Huntingdon."

One sympathizes with him when he describes his accommodations. He wrote, "In almost all of these rural cots I am under the necessity of sleeping in the same room with all the family. It seems indelicate, at least new, to strip, surrounded by different ages and sexes, and to rise in the morning in the blaze of day with the eyes of at least one...female searching out subjects for remark."

The meals varied from home to home. One menu he described consisted of a breakfast of potatoes and huckleberry pie with tea boiled in a dinner pot holding between ten to fifteen gallons of liquid. The usual fare, however, was milk, bread and butter. Frequently, supper consisted of paste and milk, the former being made of boiled milk which had thickened. When hunting was successful, there were stews, and during the summer wild fruits and berries.

When his frontier travels ended, Fithian returned to Philadelphia, eager for news of the war between the colonies and England. He wrote prophetically of America, "Thy Commerce and Thy Wealth and Power are yet to rule the Globe...Perhaps before the present Century is quite filled up, we shall have towns overlooking the banks of the Pacific Ocean."

Fithian became an active participant in the Revolution, joining the North Jersey Battalion on June 14, 1776. He died of dysentery on October 8th in Harlem Heights, a great loss to the church and country.

In 1775, Path Valley's first permanent pastor arrived. Reverend Samuel Dougal came from Scotland. He was ordained and installed on October 9, 1775 at a Presbytery meeting held at the Upper Path Valley Presbyterian Church. Dougal's background includes a dramatic story. Apparently, he was born in 1744 and named Samuel MacDougal. He attended college at Edinburgh. While there, his close friend fell in love with the daughter of a lord. The father did not approve of the match and forbade his daughter from seeing the young man. MacDougal helped his friend develop a plan for the couple to make their escape. Unfortunately, the lady's maid betrayed her trust and informed her father who gathered together a posse and gave chase, overtaking them. He fired his gun, intending to hit the prospective groom, but instead killed his daughter.

Samuel MacDougal could never forgive himself for taking part in the scheme and fled to America, dropping the prefix Mac to his name. After paying for his passage, he had very little money. He found employment in a land office in Philadelphia and later entered seminary, where he studied for ministry in the Presbyterian Church.

Rev. Dougal married Mary J. Wilson of Harrisburg in 1774. A talented and cultured woman, she played the violin beautifully. Their home was a center of culture and charity in Path Valley. Anyone in trouble was always welcomed. They and their eight children (James, John, David, Mary, Sarah, Samuel, Ann and Rachel) lived on the six hundred acre farm Rev. Dougal owned in Amberson Valley not far from Spring Run.

Prior to 1779, Rev. Dougal served the Upper Path Valley Presbyterian Church in Spring Run, the Lower Path Valley Presbyterian Church in Fannettsburg and the Upper Tuscarora Presbyterian Church near Waterloo in Juniata County. When the Path Valley churches offered him an income sufficient to support his family, he resigned from the Upper Tuscarora Presbyterian Church. The offer of 100 British pounds and 100 bushels of wheat was considered "munificent" for those days. One hundred pounds was equivalent to about $266 in Pennsylvania currency. Land was cheap, and Samuel Dougal, being a wise manager, was able to buy acreage.

The eldest son, James Dougal, received a good education and taught school. He remained in the valley, married and became an elder in the Upper Path Valley Presbyterian Church. According to some resources, he started the first Sunday School.

Rev. Dougal was a "man of the people." Warm and gentle, he reached out to all, and welcomed German families who were now coming into the valley. His style of preaching was "plain and simple." He served the churches of Path Valley for fifteen years during a formative time. In 1790, he died at the age of forty-six.

One interesting footnote to his life foreshadowed things to come. Like others in Path Valley, Rev. Dougal owned two slaves, Sambo and Dinah.

Before he died, he gave them their freedom and a little home of their own in Spring Run where they lived for many years.

Meanwhile, the Presbyterians of Path Valley continued to grow in number, practice their faith, read their Bibles, and train their children in the ways of the Lord. Other denominations would follow after the Revolution.

REVOLUTION

CHAPTER FIVE

A S THE YEARS WENT BY, the atmosphere became tense. Disquieting news was brought by horseback and spread by word of mouth. Even in remote homesteads, anger grew as bitter memories over past British injustices began to feed the present unrest. British, Indians, and colonists formed a triangle of conflict.

The colonists became more frustrated as England imposed one tax after another. The phrase, "No taxation without representation," became a rallying cry. In 1765, the Stamp Act was passed. It imposed a tax on paper which increased the cost of most business transactions. By 1767, in response to colonial protests, the Stamp Act was repealed, but the Townshend Acts which included import duties on glass, lead, paints, paper and tea was levied. British warships arrived in Boston to support the customs officials who were to collect these taxes. Later, they went off duty in the face of opposition.

A number of "tea parties" took place in New Jersey, New York, and an attempt was made in Philadelphia, but the captain of the British ship was wise enough to retreat back down the Delaware River. The most famous one, however, occurred in Boston where fifty "Indians" boarded a British ship and burst open 343 chests of tea, emptying them into the harbor. The Townshend Act was repealed in April of 1770.

"Sons of Liberty" were beginning to organize in the colonies as early as October 1765. In 1770, a Boston mob confronted British soldiers and there was gunfire. Three colonists were killed; two were mortally wounded.

In the altercations between colonists and British government that followed, radical changes took place in the political structure of Massachusetts. Royal officials were sheltered from legal suits in colonial courts. The king appointed members of council, the chief justice and superior judges. Only the royal governor could call town meetings and set agendas. Before it was over, the English parliament proposed transporting colonial malcontents to England for trial without jury. Clearly, the colonists were losing their rights and colonial opposition to British policies continued.

FIRST REBEL

In central Pennsylvania, a confrontation between the British and colonists which indirectly involved the Indians, earned James Smith, a native of Fort Loudon, the title of the "First Rebel." In May 1755, while James Smith was part of a crew engaged in building a road over the mountains to Fort Duquesne, he was captured by a group of Indians and forced to run the gauntlet. Displaying great stamina and will power, he survived and was adopted by the Indians. During this time, Smith learned to appreciate Indian traits. After five-and-a-half years, Smith made his escape, returned home, married and settled with his new bride in a cabin near Fort Loudon.

Indian raids became a major issue in 1763. Burning cabins and barns lit up the night sky and people were either killed or carried off. Out of desperation, a group of settlers collected enough money to pay for a company of riflemen. Smith was appointed captain. Smith wrote, "As we enlisted our men, we dressed them in Indian manner with breech-clouts, leggins, and moccasins, painting their faces red and black like Indian warriors." The men were nicknamed the "Black Boys." Smith said, "I taught them the Indian discipline, rather than that of the British soldiers." The "Black Boys" became skilled in making surprise attacks, and "succeeded beyond expectation in defending the frontiers."

On March 1, 1765, a powerful trading company in Philadelphia, Baynton, Wharton and Morgan, loaded goods valued around 3,000 pounds, a tremendous investment, on the backs of about 80 pack horses. The company had a license from the colony to carry on trade with the Indians, exchanging scalping knives, tomahawks, lead, and other items for furs and skins. The people on the frontier were alarmed. If Indians were equipped with tomahawks, scalping knives and guns, the lives of the settlers would be further endangered.

Justice William Duffield and a company of men met the traders to reason with them. Some say Duffield's group followed the packers over North Mountain to Great Cove. The traders, however, "made game" of what was said.

Since reasoning was not working, Smith came up with an alternate plan. He and ten of his painted warriors waylaid the packers near Sideling Hill, climbed trees, and started firing. Some of the pack horses were hit. In the midst of the fray, one trader asked, "Gentlemen, what would you have us do?" Smith shouted, "Collect all your loads and put them in one place." A great bonfire followed. The packers and their personal belongings were safe, but a major investment had gone up in flames and was now a pile of ashes. Needless to say, there were repercussions.

Returning to Fort Loudon, the traders complained bitterly to the British Commander. Soldiers were dispatched and accompanied by the traders, searched for the "Indians" without reporting to the local magistrate. They took a number of innocent prisoners and confined them in the guard-house at Fort Loudon.

Smith quickly gathered three hundred colonial riflemen, marched to the fort and camped on a hill. He reported, "It was not long before we had captured more than double as many British as they had of our people in the guard-house." A flag of truce was sent by the British Captain Grant, and the captives were freed in a prisoner exchange. Unfortunately, Captain Grant retained the rifles taken from his prisoners. On November 16, 1765, one hundred men surrounded the fort, demanding the return of the guns. Captain Grant was held hostage until the exchange took place. Unfortunately clashes continued.

On May 6, Joseph Spears brought a pack horse train to Fort Loudon loaded with many items, including barrels of rum, which often incited Indians to go on the warpath. Again, Smith's "Black Boys" took action to protect the settlers. One trader managed to alert the soldiers at the Fort. In the skirmish that followed, Smith was wounded and taken prisoner. When the British soldiers faced seventy-five angry settlers, they released him.

Smith and the "Black Boys" continued to prevent any pack train from crossing the mountains with goods that might arm or encourage Indians to attack. As Smith later admitted, "The king's troops, and our party, had now got entirely out of the channel of the civil law, and many unjustifiable things were done by both parties." He became convinced more than ever of the need for civil law in order to "govern mankind." Smith fought in the Revolution and later became a member of the Continental Congress. Known as the "First Rebel," it was he who was among the first to take action against the British.

GROWING RESISTANCE

In July 1774, people of Cumberland County, of which Path Valley was a part, met at Carlisle, the county seat, to protest British taxation. John Montgomery presided and several resolutions were passed "condemning Parliament for closing the port of Boston, recommending a General Congress of the colonies, the abandonment of the use of British merchandise and finally appointing deputies for the meeting of a General Congress."

The First Continental Congress, with fifty-six delegates from all the colonies except Georgia, gathered in Philadelphia on September 5, 1774. The meeting lasted until October 26, 1774. Congress drafted a declaration of colonial rights, encouraged the formation and arming of local militia units, approved strict economic sanctions against England, and adopted ten resolutions listing the rights of colonial assemblies. Colonists were beginning to speak of themselves as Americans and were recognizing their common unity.

The war of words soon led to military action. On April 18, 1775, General Gage sent between seven and eight hundred British soldiers to destroy the colonial arms depot in Concord. Paul Revere and William Dawes, riding like the wind, warned people in outlying areas. The British regulars met armed resistance from local militiamen at Lexington where eight Americans were killed and eight wounded. The shots fired were "heard round the world."

During June, 1775, the Second Continental Congress took action to organize the American Continental Army with George Washington as commander. He assumed office in Cambridge, Massachusetts.

On July 4th, 1776, Congress, meeting in Philadelphia, formally endorsed the Declaration of Independence which contained the words, "We hold these truths to be self evident. That all men are created equal, that they are endowed by their creator with certain unalienable Rights, that among these are Life, Liberty, and the pursuit of Happiness." Some people called the document a miracle of minds coming together and the emergence of a gifted group of leaders who were well qualified to guide the fledgling group of colonies into the order of constitutional government. By August, England declared Americans in open rebellion.

TAKING UP ARMS

Troops from Cumberland County were soon ready and marched to join Washington at the siege of Boston. Captain James Chambers with four hundred men from Franklin County marched to Reading, crossed the Delaware River at Easton, the Hudson River above West Point and arrived in Boston during August.

The troops from Pennsylvania proved valuable in the battles to come. Dr. James Thacher wrote in his book, *Military Journal of the American Revolution*, "These Pennsylvanians elicited much attention." They were described as "stout and hardy yeomanry, the flower of Pennsylvania's frontiersmen and remarkable for the accuracy of their aim, striking a mark with great certainty at two hundred yards distance." At a military review, spectators watched these Pennsylvanians "advancing quickly and firing their balls into objects seven inches in diameter at a distance of 250 yards!" One person commented, "They are now stationed in our lines, and their shot have frequently proved fatal to British officers and soldiers who expose themselves to view at more than double the distance of common musket shot." Clearly these Pennsylvanians were an asset to the army.

ACTION TO THE EAST

In the spring of 1776, the British withdrew from Boston and the Continental Army took possession of the city. Washington then gave chase to the British. As the general moved his forces from one area to another, troops from Path Valley moved with him. Washington engaged the British around New York City, escaped Manhattan Island under the cover of fog, and then retreated through New Jersey after the Battle of White Plains occurred.

Before going into winter quarters at Morristown, New Jersey, Washington achieved a much needed victory. On Christmas Eve, 1776, moving under cover in the midst of a snow storm, Washington and his troops managed to cross the icy, wind swept Delaware River to surprise the British-Hessian troops celebrating Christmas in Trenton, New Jersey. They took 1,000 British and Hessian soldiers prisoner while suffering only six casualties – quite a Christmas present for the fledgling Continental Army. Peter Foreman from Path Valley was among Washington's troops that night. After the war, he lived in a log house north of Doylesburg. Even at the age of 82, he never grew weary of describing the perilous crossing and the battle that followed. After defeating the British at Princeton, Washington went into winter quarters at Morristown.

It has been said that an attempt to follow the battles in Pennsylvania and New Jersey is like "trying to nail currant jelly to a wall." While this is true, it is equally as difficult to pinpoint battles and skirmishes that broke out between the British and the colonists in many different areas, the East, the Northwest, and the South. The Americans even led an attack against a British naval station in the Bahamas. Furthermore, skirmishes between colonists, Tories and Indians in Pennsylvania make it difficult to define lines of battle.

Attempting to place individual soldiers in the correct regiment or company of the Continental Army is not easy. Records were often less than accurate and names spelled in a variety of ways. Terms of service varied greatly. Soldiers were thrust into areas where the need was greatest regardless of their outfit. Furthermore, there existed a number of categories. Militia and rangers were recruited to protect local areas, yet were called in emergencies to serve with the Continental Army.

During 1777, Washington's forces fought the British in a number of battles around Philadelphia. During this period of time militia from Path Valley were called in as reinforcements. According to fragments of family histories, Barnabas Doyle fought in the Battle of Brandywine and Chadd's Ford serving as a guard for the wounded when they were transported to Reading. John Elliott participated in the Battles of Brandywine, Paoli, and Germantown. Sylvester Doyle served as a surgeon's mate. William Amberson served as a Deputy Muster Master General on Washington's staff. Peter Geyer was hit in the leg with a musket ball and suffered a bayonet wound at Germantown. His son, also named Peter, was a drummer in the Continental Army by the age of eleven. He, too, was wounded at Germantown and was discharged in 1778. (Later, he became a stone mason in Metal.) Path Valley troops served at White Marsh, Chestnut Hill, Germantown, Paoli, and Monmouth. In 1777, some spent the winter at Valley Forge.

BATTLES IN NEW YORK

In June 1777, General Burgoyne and his British forces planned to invade the colonies from Canada, traveling down Lake Champlain and the Hudson Valley to join up with General Howe in New York. The British would then control New England, cutting it off from the rest of the colonies. Continental forces were determined to thwart this plan.

Colonel Irvine's Sixth Regiment, part of the Second Pennsylvania Battalion, was summoned to march to upstate New York and engage General Burgoyne in battle. Companies Three, Four, and Eight were from Franklin County. Company Eight under Captain Talbott was so reduced through hard service, it had to recruit new members and many were from Fannett Township.

The movements of Colonel Irvine's Sixth Regiment are complex and well beyond the scope of this work, but the following gives some idea of what our soldiers endured. Lieutenant Colonel Thomas Hartley in his *History of the Second Pennsylvania Battalion* described the situation. About fifteen hundred men were to attack Three Rivers in four places. Thompson landed his forces about nine miles above the town on the north side of the St. Lawrence, and divided his army into five divisions, one of which Irvine commanded. They moved quickly towards the town.

Problems quickly developed. Continental officers had received poor intelligence about the location of the town and the number of enemy troops. Hartley wrote,

Our men had lost their sleep for two nights, yet were in pretty good spirits. Daylight appeared and showed us to the enemy. Our guides (perhaps traitors) had led us through several windings and were rather carrying us off from the post. The General was enraged at their conduct...We endeavored to penetrate through a swamp to the town...We waded three hours through the mud, about mid-deep in general, the men fasting. We every moment expected to get through and find some good ground to form on, but were deceived...The great body of the enemy, which we knew nothing of, consisting of two or three thousand men...began furious fire...Part of Col. Irvine's division, especially the riflemen, went towards the enemy...Under the disadvantages, our men would fight: but we had no covering, no artillery, and no prospect of succeeding as the number of the enemy was so much superior to ours... The enemy in the meantime, dispatched a strong body to cut off our retreat to the boats. Colonel Irvine was not to be found. He had gone up (to the front) during very hot fire. Later, it was found he had been captured. (According to Richard Ketchum in his book, *Saratoga*, Irvine was not released until October 28, 1780.)

Hartley's description continued…

On June 9th, it was agreed upon to take passage through the enemy and we finally overtook Colonel Wayne which made the force seven hundred strong. With forced marches, surmounting every difficulty, the river was crossed and the army arrived at Sorel, Monday afternoon, June 10th. When all gathered, they were 1200 strong with about 100 to 200 missing. Some came in gradually, so it was not the great loss we had feared. Unfortunately, many became ill for the area was unhealthy. Lieutenant Colonel Hartley with 250 from Irvine's battalion went by land to Isle La Motte, scouring the country, traversing disagreeable swamps, destroying houses and mills.

These were the conditions men from Path Valley faced.

From Isle La Motte, the army took vessels and arrived at Crown Point on July 1. Although the rest of the army was moved to Fort Ticonderoga, all or part of Irvine's battalion remained at Crown Point, acting as sentinel.

During October 1777, after a series of battles, General Burgoyne was finally defeated at the Second Battle of Saratoga. He surrendered his force of 5,700 to the Americans under General Gates. After the terms of surrender had been hammered out by the two generals who had been classmates in England, the British soldiers formed in lines before the American troops. They were ready to march to Boston and then sail home after making a promise never to engage in battle on American soil.

The parade of British troops started at 2:00 pm; they were still passing by at sunset. Around 300 women marched behind the army; many of them were wives of soldiers with their children in tow. Ragtag camp followers brought up the rear, followed "by a number of bewildered deer, raccoons, and other wild animals that had been turned into pets by lonely, homesick people." Those of higher rank were nobly entertained by the American officers, many of whom were acquainted before the war.

The defeated British troops were impressed by the discipline of the Americans. One wrote, "Not a single man gave any evidence or the slightest impression of feeling hatred, mockery, malicious pleasure, or pride for our miserable fate. There was no smile of triumph. There was only silence." Several British officers had praise for "the courage and obstinacy with which the Americans fought." One added, "Those characteristics were the astonishment of everyone, and we now become fully convinced they are not that contemptible enemy we had hitherto imagined them, incapable of standing a regular engagement."

A Hessian soldier was similarly impressed. He commented, "Dame Nature has created... a handsome race." They are "so slender, fine-looking and sinewy." In Europe, a man had to be five feet tall to be accepted in the military. Americans were usually five-eight to five-ten or taller.

INDIANS TO THE WEST

Some have said that with Burgoyne's surrender, the tide turned in favor of the Americans, but there was still much to be endured. In Pennsylvania, the war was fought on two sides; colonists faced the British on the east, and the Indians on the west. At the outbreak of the Revolution, the Americans had urged the six nations of the Iroquois Confederacy to remain neutral. Two tribes remained loyal to the Americans, and members of the Tuscarora tribe fought side by side with the Americans in a number of battles. But other members of the Iroquois Confederacy took a different approach.

In May 1778, some 300 Indians began a campaign of terror. A letter written by George Woods and Thomas Smith described the situation on the Pennsylvania frontier:

> An Indian war is now raging around us in its utmost fury…A day hardly passes without hearing of some new murder…Not one man in ten is armed. We are informed there are a great number of rifles lying in

Carlisle useless…When the men were raised for the army…we procured every gun we could for their use…Our country then loudly called on us to send all the arms to camp… Now as loudly…we entreat that we may be allowed some (arms) as soon as possible, and also some ammunition.

With guns in such short supply, people often had only axes and pitchforks with which to defend themselves.

Well acquainted with their Indian foes and the danger at their back door, the first battalion of Cumberland County Militia was formed in 1777, commanded by Colonel James Dunlap. There were three companies from Franklin County, one of which originated in Path Valley and served under Captain Noah Abraham who lived near Spring Run. Militia and rangers were responsible for home protection and saw service in 1777-1778. At times, they were called to give aid to the Continental Army.

TORY TROUBLES

Indians weren't the only danger. Pennsylvania had its share of Tories who were not in sympathy with the Revolution and remained loyal to the British king. A number of Tories lived in areas west and north of Path Valley. Expecting a British victory, they began to dream of the spoils of war. They coveted the farms owned by patriot families in their own areas and in the rich valleys of the Conococheague and the Conodoguinet.

One of the Tory leaders was John Weston. Some sources say he lived in Canoe Valley, not far from Water Street. Others say Weston lived in Amberson where it was easier to make contact with British officers at Carlisle. It is possible he lived sporadically at both sites. There were five known Tories in Amberson and two in Path Valley.

According to U.J. Jones in his *History of Juniata Valley*, Weston held many secret meetings at Water Street. There plans were laid to gather a large force of Indians and Tories at Kittanning. One party would sweep through the Cove and Conococheague Valley while the other would attack Juniata Valley. The plan was to kill all male inhabitants capable of bearing arms and anyone attempting to escape. The Tories would claim the farms; the Indians would acquire personal property. They would join forces in Lancaster.

Weston did not work alone. Jacob Hare, a vicious man with a reputation for brutality, was another prominent Tory and a large landowner in Huntingdon County. One of his victims was a young man by the name of Loudenslater who was on his way to Huntingdon to enlist. Hare and a small group of Indians fired on Loudenslater, who leaving a trail of blood reached Huntingdon, living long enough to describe Hare. The same day, the Eaton family was killed and their buildings burned by Hare's party.

Tory leaders, Weston and Hare, were joined by a third leader, a man named Alexander McKee from Amberson Valley. Like Weston, he too was in contact with the British in Philadelphia and Detroit as well as in Carlisle where some were incarcerated.

Rumors ran rampant as Tory neighbors whispered to each other about the uprising to come. As if to confirm suspicions, news came from Fort Pitt that Alexander McKee, Simon Girty, and Matthew Elliott, long suspected of holding Tory sympathies, had fled from their posts and gone over to the British and Indians.

On the night of April 16, 1778, many men disappeared from settlements to the west. Family members said, "They've gone hunting," but their neighbors were suspicious. Michael Cryder, a loyal patriot and owner of a mill several miles above Standing Stone, discovered his hired man, Pierce, had disappeared. On the door of Cryder's mill was a written statement, "This mill belongs to General Howe." Fearful for the safety of her patriot friends, Pierce's wife took action. Those in sympathy with the Tory movements were to display tiny little flags devised for identification. She insisted her friend, Mrs. Cryder, do so. The secret was out! Weston had ordered all Tories to Sinking Valley to form a company.

News traveled fast. Captain Thomas Blair of Path Valley learned that Tories were to meet Weston, McKee, and others and then proceed to Kittanning. Intent on disrupting the Tory plan, Captain Blair headed west with about twenty Rangers from Path Valley and Blair's Mills. He picked up more recruits as he traveled. Eventually, Blair's group had about 45 men. They hurried along the Kittanning Trail, trying to catch up with Weston.

What happened next was what many would call an act of God. Weston had ordered Tories to Sinking Valley to form a company while he went on to Kittanning. There he and Hare entered an Indian town where they were received with courtesy. A dozen armed warriors joined Weston and Hare and started the journey east to Sinking Valley.

The two white men walked in advance. Some say Weston, trying to make a fine appearance, gave the order to present arms. In a moment of misunderstanding, the Indians shot Weston and scalped him! Realizing what they had done, the warriors turned and raced home to await attack.

When the Tories who had gathered in Sinking Valley heard the news, they fled. Some headed for Baltimore to find a way to England. Weston's brother Robert, turned himself in to Captain John McDonald. According to the story, his brother John had asked him to go hunting. Soon, they had met up with McKee, Hare and around 31 men. They urged him to go to Kittanning and join the Tories and Indians, promising him 300 acres when they'd achieved victory. If he refused, they said, he would be hanged or banished.

Meanwhile, Captain Blair and his men continued the chase. They came upon two of Weston's Tories. Blair's men wanted to shoot them, but Blair granted their plea for life. After the Tories had scattered, Blair ordered his men to march for home.

Since Robert Weston had implicated a man named Hess, they stopped to pay a visit. Finding him at home, they took him to the neighboring woods for punishment. Rope was scarce so the Rangers bent a sapling, fastened the smaller branches around his neck, and then released the sapling. He was frightened but not injured. Strangely enough, Hess later enlisted in the Rangers and was a loyal American the rest of his life.

Later, word passed rapidly through upper Path Valley that Jacob Hare had stopped at the house of Nathaniel Paul about three miles from Concord. A great crowd gathered. Among those present were Richard and Thomas Morrow, William McMullin, William Kelly, Edward Kelly, Thomas Askey,

James Lauthers, Matthew Crumsby, William Darlington, and a man named Shoemaker. Some sources also include the name of Captain Blair. Apparently, when hanging was discussed, Blair, a good Presbyterian, said murder was not the answer.

After much debate, it was decided Hare's ears should be cropped. Darlington secured "a case-knife and hacked it to a saw-like edge on an old iron pot." Two men held Hare while both of his ears were sawed off close to his head. He was then given his freedom and told never to return. It was rumored he became a minister in either Ohio or Kentucky. The mother-in-law of Senator Creswell of Hollidaysburg remembered seeing Hare when she was quite young. "He wore his hair long," she said.

Another source tells of a spy from Locke Valley near Shade Gap who came through the Gap carrying news to the British in Philadelphia. Upon his return, he stopped in Path Valley where he slept on Andrew Campbell's porch. Campbell's son rounded up the neighbors who came and removed his ears. It was reported he "yelled so loud he could be heard across the fields." A rude awakening if true!

WOMEN SOLDIERS

While these events were occurring at home, families were concerned about members fighting the British on far away battlefields. In some cases, women followed loved ones and took part in the actual fighting. Everyone is familiar with the heroine, "Molly Pitcher," whose real name was Mary Hays McCauly. Her actions at the Battle of Monmouth in New Jersey made her famous. Molly carried water to cool hot guns and parched throats, and frequently tended the wounded. During the Battle of Monmouth, she found her husband wounded and the gun he was manning about to be withdrawn because the crew was too depleted to fight. Molly quickly stepped forward and manned the gun. General Washington issued her a "warrant" as a noncommissioned officer and she became known as "Sergeant Molly." She is buried at Carlisle.

Fewer people know about Margaret Cochran Corbin from Lurgan. She was married to John Corbin who served as a gunner in the Pennsylvania Artillery. During the battle at Fort Washington, John was killed while manning his gun. Since there was no one to replace him, Margaret stepped up and took her husband's place. She helped load and fire the gun until she herself was severely wounded. Congress later granted her a pension equal to half the pay of a soldier and requested "that she now receive, out of the public stores, one suit of clothes or the value thereof in money." This was, in all likelihood, one of the first military pensions granted to a woman by Congress.

Margaret Goyer, related to the Miller family of Path Valley, also gained recognition for her courage in battle. During the Revolution, her husband John served as a soldier and Margaret as a washerwoman for the officers. Their son, (also named John) age twelve, served as a drummer boy. When her husband was shot, Margaret picked up his musket and fought through the battle. Margaret Goyer lived to be 103 and also drew a pension for her service in the Revolution. Eventually, she made her home in Carlisle.

MERCHANTS AND MINISTERS

Not all fighting was done with guns. Ephraim Blaine, whose family settled in Perry County near the town that now bears his name, organized millers and farmers who were sympathetic to the Continentals to send supplies. Getting provisions to Washington's troops was difficult, particularly at Valley Forge. Blaine obtained teamsters and financed the supply trains. Without such shipments of food and ammunition, the war would have been lost.

Meanwhile, ministers played an important role in recruiting soldiers. At the Rocky Spring Presbyterian Church near Chambersburg, Rev. John Craighead who had a "deep aversion to tyranny and oppression" was preaching powerful sermons about the wrongs suffered at the hands of the British and the duty of Americans to right them. According to the story, an anguished mother who had lost her son in the war called out one Sunday, "Quit talking and go yourself!" At dawn the next morning, Rev. Craighead and his parishioners gathered. After solemn prayers, gray-headed men and boys so young they were still trying to grow beards marched off with Craighead to join General Washington in New Jersey. After they disappeared from sight, the women and children returned home determined to do their part for the cause by taking over the duties of home.

Rev. Craighead was not the only pastor who marched off to war taking part of the congregation with him. Rev. John Woodfull of Leacock Presbyterian Church in Lancaster County persuaded every able-bodied man from his church to go with him. Rev. John King of Mercersburg, Rev. George Duffield of Carlisle, and Rev. Robert Cooper of Middle Spring were also part of the fighting force.

A Rev. William Foster of Donegal Presbytery was such a formidable enemy that General Howe sent a group of light horsemen from Delaware to kidnap and silence him. Warned, the congregation rallied and whipped the British who slunk back to Delaware.

One Englishman said he would "rather meet a battalion of soldiers than one Presbyterian who believed he was doing the will of God." In the English parliament, Horace Walpole remarked, "There is no use crying about it. Cousin America has run off with a Presbyterian parson, and that is the end of it."

VICTORY AND A NEW NATION

The Revolution was not won until the South was cleared of the British. General Green replaced General Gates and began a guerilla campaign against the British which finally turned the tide. On Kings Mountain in North Carolina during October 1780, a British force of 1,100 men was captured by 900 American frontiersmen. Finally, in August of 1781, the Americans laid siege to General Cornwallis and his troops at Yorktown, Virginia. Some Path Valley men were probably among the troops that witnessed the British surrender in October 1781.

In February 1782, Parliament enacted legislation empowering the British crown to negotiate peace with the United States. In November of the same year, a preliminary peace treaty was drawn up. Finally, in April 1783, peace was formally declared by Congress.

Some soldiers who had come with the British to fight the Americans decided to stay. Dorothy Crouse shared the story of one of her ancestors, Peter Crouse. When it came time to return, he wasn't sure. "I don't think I will go home. Why they say down Philadelphia way there are mile long markets with counters loaded with plump chickens and sausages, crisp fresh bread and buns fragrant with cinnamon, with cherries and peas and other vegetables in season." Gasping for breath he went on, "And snug inns where a man can sit before the fire and down his pot of liquor or turn in between fresh lavender-scented sheets. Ah, that would be a good life. Why go back?" A shocked companion said, "Why? It's the land of your birth!" "But if I stay," said Peter, "I have a plot of land. Soon I will have plump chickens and sausages and crisp fresh bread. More than I can ever have in Germany. Why not stay?" He did. And so did many others.

The end of the Revolution brought celebrations. Free and independent citizens dreamed of a new future. July 4th celebrations were plentiful. Usually, a platform was erected in the woods and decorated with evergreens. From the local church or school, men, women, and children processed to the sound of "Yankee Doodle" played by fife and drum. The Declaration of Independence was read and speeches by dignitaries or recitations by children followed. Pie, cake, butter rolls, and gingerbread were washed down by spring water or "small beer."

The war had ended, but the thirteen colonies now faced the rigorous work of becoming a nation. In November of 1777, Congress had endorsed the Articles of Confederation which were then presented to the colonies for their approval. By July 1778, Pennsylvania delegates had endorsed the Articles of Confederation as other colonies did in subsequent months.

Reforms were made to create a more just and representative government. Governors were now chosen by the people not by the Crown. Members of the upper chambers of legislatures were now elected not appointed. Previously in Pennsylvania, only men who owned a certain amount of land had the right to vote. Now, any male taxpayer could vote. Previously, only the three counties in the east had representatives, now the western part of the state was represented.

Loyalists, many of whom had been major property owners, departed en masse. As one historian wrote, "Following their departure the homely, hard-working farmers, shopkeepers, and artisans were free to create a civilization after their own hearts...Everybody was counted equal, and everybody was in a hurry." Class distinctions began to disappear, especially in Pennsylvania.

Still, the government was not really effective in bringing the former colonies together as a nation. That would require yet more work. The "Articles of Confederation" was simply a "league of friendship," and would soon prove inadequate. There was no provision for a true national executive or national system of courts. Congress consisted of one house in which each state had a single vote. It could not levy taxes, enlist troops, punish men who broke the law, or compel the states to observe treaties it made with other countries. In fact, it could not raise enough money to carry on the functions of government or pay interest on the national debt.

Finally, a convention was called. Fifty-five delegates represented their states. Approximately half were college graduates; many were lawyers. Laying aside the deficient Confederation, the delegates began work on a constitution. All agreed that there should be three distinct branches of government. The legislative, executive, and judicial powers were intended to be balanced so that no branch could gain control. Although the three branches were independent, the power of each was to be held in check by the others. In September 1787, the Constitutional Convention endorsed the final form of the constitution. Pennsylvania was the second state to ratify the document. Questions persisted. Would it work? Would other states ratify it?

Finally, the new government was in operation. In 1789, George Washington was elected President and John Adams, Vice President. George Washington stood on the balcony of Federal Hall in New York City and took the oath of office. A thunderous shout arose, "Long live George Washington, President of the United States!" The theme was "Be United - Be Americans!"

Amid controversies and testing, the country grew "sturdily" in the years that followed. Path Valley's earliest settlers were known for their involvement in politics. They were informed. They debated issues. Before a hotly-contested election, a horseback rider often appeared, blowing his horn to gather people. Papers, circulars, and political flyers were distributed by various political parties. Elections were loudly disputed and victories highly celebrated. It was said men suffered from laryngitis for days. Path Valley sent forth an inordinate number of people who became active in politics on both the state and the national level.

2ⁿᵈ PENNSYLVANIA BATTALION

SIXTH REGIMENT

IRVINE'S REGIMENT

Company 3

Captain– Abraham Smith, commissioned January 9, 1776
First Lieutenant– Robert White
Second Lieutenants– John Alexander, Andrew Irvine
Ensigns– Samuel Montgomery, Samuel Kennedy
Sergeants– John Beatty, Samuel Hamilton, Hugh Foster, William Scott, William Burke
Corporals– William Burke, George Standley, John Moore, William Campbell, Seth Richey, William McCormick, William Drennon, William Cochran (fifer), John Fannon

Privates– David Armor, John Brown, Patrick Brown, John Blakeley, John Brannon, Philip Boyle, Josiah Cochran, Robert Craighead, Anthony Greevy, William Cochran, James Dunlap, Thomas Drennon, William Downey, Hugh Drennon, Daniel Divinney, Pat Fleming, William Gwin, Alexander Gordon, Robert Gregg, Thomas Higgins, James Holliday, Thomas Holmes, John Hendricks, Benjamin Ishmail, Robert Jarrett, Thomas Johnson, Samuel Love, George Lucas, Nicholas Little, James Lowrey, Daniel McKusick, John McCollam, William McCormick, Michael McGarea, Bryan McLaughlin, John McFetridge, Michael McMullin, James McKissock, Adam McBreas, John McDowell, Samuel McBrea, Robert McIlno, Alexander McKenny, John McKingham, John Montgonery, Alexander Moore, Robert Miller, Hugh Milligan, Moses Powell, Nathan Points, John Rannell, Seth Richey, Patrick Rogers, John Rannell Jr., Peter Runey, Alexander Reid, Borthal Roharty, Thomas Smith, Patrick Silvers, Thomas Scott, George Simpson, Robert Swinie, John Stoops, Ad Shearer, William Stitt, Peter Sheran, Charles Tipper, John Todd, Mich White, James White, John Wilson, John Young

Company No. 4

Captain– William Rippey
First Lieutenants– William Alexander, Alexander Parker
Second Lieutenant– John Brooks
Ensign– William Lusk
Sergeants– John Hughes, Robert Watt, John McClelland, William Anderson
Corporals– William Gibbs, Jeremiah McKibben, James McCulloh, George Gordon, Nath Stevenson, William Richards (fifer), Daniel Peterson (drummer)

Privates– Jacob Anderson, Robert Barckley, Bernerd Burns, Robert Caskey, Henry Cartright, Robert Cortney, Jacob Christyardinger, Benjamin Cochran, Hugh Call, John Collins, William Dougherty, John Davison, Joseph Devine, Anthony Dawson, Thomas Dyke, James Finerty, Hugh Forsyth, Hugh Ferguson, Thomas Falls, William George, Henry Girden, Thomas Gell, Jacob Glouse, Than Hemphill, Robert Haslet, John Hendry, William Henderson, James Hervey, Cumberland Hamilton, Neal Hardon, George Hewitt, Robert Irvine, Jacob Justice, John Johnston, Christopher Kechler, Francis Kain, John Kelly, William Lowry, Daniel Lavery, David Linsey, James Lynch, John Madden, Josiah McCall, John McMicheal, James McComb, William McInyre, John Moore, James Mullin, Thomas McCall, Philip Melon, Alexander McNichols, James McCoy, James McCon, David McClain, John McDonell, Daniel McClain

Company No. 8

Captain– Jeremiah Talbott
First Lieutenant– John McDonald
Second Lieutenant– Alexander Brown
Ensign– William Graham
Sergeants– John McCollam, John Wilson, James Cupples, Samuel Mitchell

Corporals– William Campbell, Robert Hunter, John Chain, John Reniston, John Milton (drummer), John Killin (fifer)

Privates– Robert Asten, John Bardley, William Black, John Church, George Caghren, Francis Clark, Robert Carnahan, Charles Conna, John Campbell, Joseph Chambers, John Dinning, William Evans, John Faulkner, Hugh Fairess, James Gardner, Daniel Gibson, William Heaslett, John Heatherington, Duke Handlon, John Higgens, Kern Kelley, Stephen Lyon, Jacob Lewis, Hugh Lilley, John Marten, Robert Mollon, Benjamin Morrison, James McFarlan, Charles McRoun, Archibald McDonald, Matthew McConnell, Thomas McCreary, Charles McMullen, Thomas Mitchell, Charles Marry, Patrick Marry, Able Morgan, Archibald Nickel, Andrew Pinkerton, Samuel Power, John Pollock, James Quarre, William Shaw, Mike Sesalo, John Shoemaker, James Sloan, John Totton, John Thompson, Hugh Thompson, William White, John White, John Welch, Robert Watson, Isaac Wiley

In April 1777, Capt. Talbott's company had been so reduced by hard service that the following recruits were added:

Thomas Aston, William Atrican, Gilbert Berryhill, Michael Black, Pat Boyle, John Brown, Michael Brown, Robert Burns, William Campbell, Conrad Carcass, Hugh Cassidy, John Cavenaugh, Charles Conner, George Corohan, John Crowl, Patrick Doyle, Thomas Dunn, John Feaghander, John Fergeson, John Foster, William Foster, John Fullerton, James Garlant, William Gibbs, Patrick Guinn, Edward Hart, Robert Hunter, John Johnson, John Kellenough, Charles Kelley, James Loe, William McCalley, Daniel McCartney, John McCullum, Patrick McCullum, Michael McDaufer, William McDonald, Andrew McGahey, Barney McGilligen, John McKinley, Patrick McKinley, John Milton, Patrick Murrey, Francis O'Harrah, Phelix O'Neal, John Robinson, James Rolls, Christopher Row, Mike Sesalo, William Shaw, Thomas Sherry, Isaac Shockey, John Shoemaker, Michael Siteler, John Smith, John Smith (Tanner), Peter Smith, Hugh Thompson, Henry Vaughan, Joseph West, Tomas Whitely, John Wilson

BATTALION OF CUMBERLAND COUNTY MILITIA

This battalion was commanded by Colonel James Dunlap and Lieutenant Colonel Robert Culbertson. There were three companies. Captain Noah Abraham commanded a company from Path Valley.

Captain– Noah Abraham
First Lieutenant– Archibald Elliott
Second Lieutenant– Samuel Walker
Sergeants– James McConnaughy, Joseph Noble, Robert McConnell, Thomas Clark

Privates– Robert Alexander, James Alexander, David Armstrong, John Adams, William Adams, James Allen, John Brown, Allen Brown, James Boggs, Nathanael Bryan, William Buchanan, John Bell, Samuel Campbell, James Carmady, Daniel Colbert, William Cortz, John Canady, Patrick Davidson, Henry Delmer, Patrick Dougherty, Andrew Douglas Sr., George Dixson, William Elliott, Francis Elliott, Samuel Elder, Abram Elder, Samuel Elder, George Farmer, Charles Gibson, William Harvey, James Harvey, Henderson Harvey, James Howe, Andrew Hemphill, Alexander Hopper, Adam Humberg, John Johnson, Joseph Kilgore, Alex. Long, Hugh McCurdy, Alexander McConell, James Mitchell, John McLellan Jr., Samuel Mears, James Mackey, Robert McGuire, Henry McGee, John Mackey, John Montgomery, John McLellan, Alexander Mear, Samuel McCauley, James McLellan, William McLellan, William McIbbins, John Means, Nathan McColley, James Montgomery, Alex Meor, James Nealy, David Neal, James Park, William Wright, Robert Walker, Samuel Watson, William Woodrow, Henry Varner

In 1779, a company recruited from Path Valley was mustered into the service, and sent west to quell an Indian disturbance. This was Capt. Noah Abraham's Company.

First Lieutenant– Nathaniel Stevenson
Second Lieutenant– Adam Harman
Sergeants– Joseph Ferguson, Campbell Lefever, James Hamilton, John Roach.

Privates– Daniel Colbert, Neal Dougherty, Frederick Dougherty, Patrick Dougherty, Thomas Knox, Daniel Lavrey, William Love, Redmond McDonough, Mathias Maers, John Maghan, John Millison, James Megraw, Isaac Miner, James Russell, John Robinson, James Ray William Walker

NAMES THAT APPEAR ON THE MONUMENT AT THE AMERICAN LEGION

Noah Abraham (Capt.), John Adams, William Adams, James Allen, James Alexander, Robert Alexander, David Armstrong, John Bell, James Boggs, Allen Brown, John Brown, Nathaniel Bryan, Samuel Campbell, James Canada, John Canada, William Carty, Thomas Clark, David Colbert, Patrick Davidson, Harry Delmer, George Dixon, Patrick Dougherty, Alex Douglas, Andrew Douglas, Abram Elder, David Elder, Samuel Elder, Archibald Elliot (Lt.), Francis Elliot, William Elliot, George Farmer, James Fegan, John Flickinger (Lt. Col.), John Garver, Charles Gibson, Jacob Guyer, John Harmin, James Harvey, William Harvey, Andrew Hemphill, Alex Hopper, James Howe, Henderson Hawer, Adam Humburg, John Johnson, Alex Long, John Mackey, Samuel McCauley, Nathan McColley, James McConaughy, Robert McConnell, Hugh McCurdy, Harry McGee, Robert McGuire, William McIbbons, James McLelland, John McLelland, William McLelland, John Means, Samuel Means, James Mitchell, James Montgomery, David Neal, James Nealy, Joseph Noble, James Park, George Shearer, John Steward, Henry Varner, Robert Walker, Samuel Walker, Samuel Woodward, William Woodward, William Wright

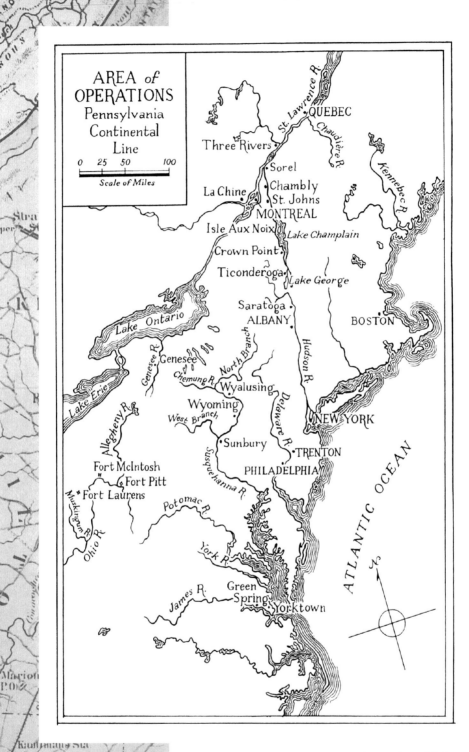

AREA of
OPERATIONS
Pennsylvania
Continental
Line

0   25   50   100
Scale of Miles

Areas in which
Path Valley soldiers served.

BUILDING A NATION

CHAPTER SIX

P RIOR TO THE REVOLUTION, travel was for the most part confined to trails accommodating foot traffic and pack horses. General Henry Bouquet, a British officer, described a road from Fort Loudon to Cowan's Gap and Fort Littleton. "Of all roads where it is possible for a wagon to go, this is the worst!" Rains had washed all the earth from the rocky roadbed which was solid only in parts, and full of sharp stones. Wagons broke down and horses lost shoes. "Wretched state of affairs!" declared Bouquet in disgust.

Indian paths often littered with fallen trees and brush ran the length of the valley. A prominent trail crossed the valley from Fannettsburg through Cowan's Gap. Farther up the valley, Conrad Weiser and his travelers used a trail that crossed from Amberson to Doylesburg on their way to negotiate with Indian tribes in the west. Where the terrain allowed, people and horses broke through the brush and created a new path.

In 1785, an act of the Pennsylvania Assembly set aside the equivalent of six hundred pounds of gold or silver ($1,600) to construct a much-needed road from Shippensburg to Burnt Cabins, later called Three Mountain Road. The plan called for a road of such grade that a team of four horses could pull a load of 2,000 pounds up either side of the mountain. Two hundred pounds were all a pack horse could carry. John Skinner won the contract from the governor and executive council and began work on the road which was to be finished on or before November 25, 1787.

Three Mountain Road bore heavy traffic and was used by pack horses as well as drovers who were responsible for delivering horses, mules, cattle, hogs, and turkeys to New York and Philadelphia markets. Drovers were expected to cover eleven miles a day, and three times that distance on the return trip.

With road traffic came taverns which provided work for both men and women. Taverns supplied travelers with food and refreshment as well as pasturing, stabling, and feed for their horses. Blacksmiths for shoeing and other metalwork, colliers to make and sell charcoal, and carpenters to repair wagons were among the trades in demand.

In 1800, as reported in a newspaper article, a brave female traveler, Miss Hastings, in the company of others, made her wagon trip over the Three Mountain Road. After eating at Skinner's Inn in Horse Valley, she described the area as a "wilderness that seems to be excluded from all prospect of civilized life; it has the appearance of Solitude and Terror, beyond anything of my imagination." Her description of Fannettsburg was gentler. "This little village of Fannettsburg is situated in the midst of a lovely valley called, 'The Path.' The inhabitants seem to enjoy a degree of luxurious plenty, and our hosts are really polite folk." Upon leaving Fannettsburg, Miss Hastings commented that the inn was so crowded their party decided to cook breakfast on the way, but later her diary described the difficulties of climbing the Tuscarora Mountain in the rain. "The road slippery - almost impossible to keep our feet on the good earth."

In June of 1802, another traveler, Francois Andre Michaux, described Fannettsburg as a settlement of thirty houses on both sides of the road and twenty plantations covering two to three hundred acres of woody land each with several acres cleared. Michaux then wrote, "In this part of Pennsylvania, every individual is content with cultivating a sufficiency for himself and family. The larger family a man has capable of assisting him, the greater independence he enjoys. This is one of the principal causes of the rapid progress that population makes in the United States."

The following year, in his *Journal of a Tour*, Thaddeus Mason Harris commented that in Fannettsburg all the houses were built of hewn logs "with the exception of the inn, a handsome edifice of limestone."

Writing in the winter of 1807, F. Cumings gave a full description of the Skinner Tavern.

> At four o'clock, I stopped at Skinners where at my particular request I was gratified with hasty pudding or mush with plenty of good milk and apple pie for supper. My host was born near Woodbridge in Jersey... Mrs. Skinner was confined to her bed in an advanced stage of consumption; I recommended her inhaling the steam of melted rosin and beeswax, and wrote directions for her accordingly. When I retired to rest, I had once more the luxury of clean sheets and a good bed.

Further entries described the scenery two miles from the Skinner Tavern. Looking down from the top of the mountain on the farms and village of Fannettsburg, he waxed eloquently saying, "Its beauty reminded him of Switzerland." Cumings described his journey over Tuscarora Mountain in less elegant terms. "In many places it was like glass from the freezing of the snow after a partial thaw...The views of the valley behind were very fine...but the view to the west was cheerless and gloomy over a broken and mountainous country covered with forests of dark and somber pine." Nevertheless, Cummings and his companions found a tavern farther west where "the whole floor was filled with people wrapped in their blankets around a roaring fire... laughing, joking, romping!" Unfortunately for some guests, bedding was not supplied. Whiskey was the comfort drink which seemed to alleviate all ailments and discomforts.

Among the famous who crossed the mountain were Marcus and Narcissa Whitman and their companions, the Spaulding's, missionaries to the Indians in the Oregon territory. Narcissa Whitman and Mrs. Spaulding were the first women to cross the Rockies. Narcissa was known for her cheerful and graceful spirit. As one traveler reported, "Narcissa could make a meal in the wilderness seem like a fancy tea in New England." When they passed through Fannettsburg, they were traveling by wagon and saddle en route to Pittsburgh.

For many, the most exciting moment was provided by the appearance of President George Washington on the Three Mountain Road during the Whiskey Rebellion in 1794. During the Revolution, an excise tax of six pence had been placed on every gallon of whiskey bringing in much needed revenue. The tax was a hardship on those who distilled their grain into whiskey which was easily transported unlike other products from the farm. Through selling whiskey farmers could earn money to purchase salt, iron and other articles necessary for carrying on agricultural pursuits.

On October 22, Washington crossed the Tuscarora Mountain coming from Bedford and paused at Fannettsburg where he was met with a hearty welcome. Undoubtedly, there were veterans of the Revolution who had fought by his side. The extent of his visit is not known, but it is a matter of record that he stayed at the Skinner Tavern in Horse Valley, sometimes called Half Way Tavern. According to local sources, eighteen-year-old Jacob Shearer asked Washington's advice about desirable places to settle in the West. He may have been disappointed when President Washington advised him to go over the mountain to Path Valley.

Washington seemed well pleased with the country and wrote in a letter to Alexander Hamilton, "Thus far I have proceeded without accident to man, horse, or carriage altho' the latter has had wherewith to try its goodness, especially in ascending the North Mountain from Skinner's by a wrong road…next to impassable by neglect." Apparently, Washington got lost and in a letter to John Adams explained that he "returned to Skinner's for some more of his good whiskey." Finally, he and his party reached Strasburg, a busy little town where wagons and horses often filled the road, making it difficult to pass through.

Although members of Congress from districts in western Pennsylvania had "pleaded, talked and voted in vain to prevent its passage," the excise tax on whiskey had become the law of the land after the Revolution. At the time there were seventy-one stills in Franklin County. Fannett Township had six with a capacity ranging from ten to 100 gallons.

Thomas Jefferson thought Hamilton's excise law "odious" and expressed that opinion to Washington pointing out that resistance to it was likely. Hamilton believed in vigorous federal authority whereas Jefferson, fearing the power of monopolies, sought to give individuals more liberty.

Trouble began in Hagerstown on the court-house square where around 300 people gathered and erected a "liberty pole," a tall round pole with various flags or symbols decorating it. Three hundred militiamen arrived from Frederick and arrested 120 men. Chambersburg was also caught up in the rebellion and erected their liberty pole. Two hundred dragoons paid them a visit. Rioting spread to Harrisburg and Northumberland.

Although not all citizens of Fannettsburg were of the same opinion, one group joined the rebels and with great glee erected their own liberty pole decorated with a long red streamer blowing in the wind. Little time elapsed before a rider came into town yelling, "The advance guard of the United States troops is crossing the mountain! They'll see your liberty pole!" The pole was quickly cut down and the culprits scurried away. According to the local newspaper, those who had erected it bore the brunt of many jests over their lack of bravery.

Traveling was difficult when the Conococheague creek east of Fannettsburg ran high. One built a rough raft, waited for the water to recede or rode across on a horse. Perhaps the publicity that followed Washington on his trip encouraged the legislature to authorize $300 for the construction of two bridges, one at Fannettsburg, the other near the Skinner Tavern in Horse Valley. John Skinner and his son built both although other names have also been credited. These were the first bridges built in Franklin County.

Road building accelerated. The turnpike road from Chambersburg to Baltimore was built in 1809, followed by the turnpike to Pittsburgh in 1820 which was described as "rough and narrow filled with long lines of pack horses or broad wheeled wagon, their high bows covered with canvas and drawn by teams of six or eight horses." All Path Valley roads and roads farther north in Juniata County emptied onto these turnpikes.

In 1830, Henry R.F. Mollqitz, keeper of the North Mountain turnpike leading from Fort Loudon to McConnellsburg, recorded the following traffic: broad wheeled wagons 6,641, narrow wheeled wagons 495, single horses 761, carriages 138, two horse wagons 318, gigs 18, riding horses 3,116, draft horses 39,824, heads of cattle 5,834, sheep 2,180, hogs 1,180, carts 18. Cargoes of salt, iron, utensils, textiles, hardware, and manufactured goods were transported west while loads coming east were filled with furs and skins. To complete the picture of prosperous trade, horses often wore tinkling brass bells. Some were decorated with rosettes, pom-poms, and even ribbon tassels.

About every tenth house on the turnpike was a tavern, and some claim every fourth house in Path Valley had, at one time or another, served the same purpose. The sounds of merriment echoed through the woods at night as violins, accordions or banjos could be heard playing "Arkansas Traveler, Zip Coon, Little Brown Jug, or Turkey in the Straw." With plenty of whiskey, the hearty wagoners as well as travelers danced the Virginia reel, the hoedown, and many others.

The wagoners were described as a proud, colorful lot sporting broad-brimmed hats, beards, blue cotton shirts, plain suits of homespun wool, and bare feet sometimes slipping in and out of shoes or high leather boots. They were a noisy group, sometimes singing, sometimes arguing, and sometimes involved in brawls as they boasted of their superiority.

Upon one occasion, a wagoner demonstrated his ability to drive his animals by word of mouth as he lay flat on his back in a field. Signaling to his lead horse, six horses and the wagon passed over him safely, straddling his body. As if that were not enough, by verbal instructions he had the horses turn around and pass over him again without getting off his back. Such was the remarkable working relationship between the wagoner and his team.

Wagoners frequently demonstrated their physical strength. One wagoner loaded a 100 pound keg of nails onto his wagon by grasping the narrow lip of the keg between the fingers and thumb of one hand. Another, it was reported, unloaded a 600 pound barrel of molasses without help. Most fortified themselves with the contents of their little brown jug filled with liquid from the barrels that made up their cargoes.

The wagoners' days were long, typically beginning at 4:00 a.m. and ending at 5:00 p.m. when they pulled into a tavern, fed their horses from either a long feed trough which hung on chains at the rear of their wagon or with hay, corn, and oats provided by the tavern keeper. After supper and entertainment, they pulled in their bedding. By 10 p.m., all that could be heard was the rhythmic snoring of many men while the flames danced low in the fireplace.

The stage-coach line from Chambersburg to Pittsburgh was established in 1804. Concord coaches were advertised as a "most speedy and most pleasant means of passing from east to west." Several lines of stage-coaches departed daily for Philadelphia, Pittsburgh and Baltimore. The arrival of a coach, its driver sitting high on top with trunks loaded behind, was most exciting when rival lines converged. Horns announced their arrival as the coaches came thundering into town, their horses lathered with sweat and streamers flying. This event provided excitement for all.

It was not until the mid-eighteen hundreds that there was a stage north and south in Path Valley. In a newspaper called the *Concord Pioneer* published in 1862 by David Goshorn, a schedule for coaches running between Perrysville (Port Royal) and the Fannettsburg state line was advertised. The schedule read, "The undersigned desire to call the attention of the Public to the fact that they run a line of coaches from Perrysville to Concord and request the patronage of the traveling public. The coaches leave Perrysville every Monday, Wednesday and Friday at six o'clock a.m. and arrive at Concord same day at 4 p.m. The coaches leave Concord every Tuesday, Thursday and Saturday at 6 a.m. and arrive at Perrysville at 4 p.m." Additional information revealed a schedule for coaches leaving Concord for Fannettsburg on Tuesday, Thursday, and Saturday at 6 a.m. and returning by 12:00 p.m.. In the afternoon, the schedule included a stage run which left Fannettsburg at 2 p.m. and arrived in

Concord at 6 p.m. Travelers were assured, "The horses and coaches are good and the drivers safe. A.B. and J. Siebert, Proprietors, Concord, Pa."

Meanwhile, peddlers with large fancy wagons drawn by two horses became a regular part of the traffic. These men had regular seasonal routes. Customers came out to see new merchandise and happily parted with their money.

There were many adventures for travelers, but there was one encounter they all feared. Known as a modern Robin Hood, his name was David Lewis of Bedford. According to some sources, Lewis was born in Carlisle in 1790 and fought in the War of 1812, plundering officers and men alike. When the campaign ended, he was sent with a team of horses to return to their owner. Instead, he headed for the Allegheny Mountains, sold the team and kept the money. Lewis blamed his thievery on liquor. Fleeing to a cave, he began his career as robber and counterfeiter in the Somerset area of Pennsylvania. Apparently, his charismatic personality drew others into counterfeiting and the band came east and over the mountains to Chambersburg. Their first task was to buy suitable paper for printing bank bills from John Shryock, a paper manufacturer, but for some reason Shryock refused to sell. When he turned his back, Lewis picked up a sample and traveled south until he could find a supply of similar paper. Returning to Somerset, he and his gang manufactured different bank notes and began to distribute them throughout the area.

Later, Lewis erected a hut on South Mountain in Cumberland County and with his gang printed around one thousand dollars, passing out the bills in Strasburg, Roxbury and Fannettsburg. Too free with the counterfeit money, Lewis landed in jail. Pardoned at the end of the year, he returned home and resumed his activities.

Despite Lewis' fearsome reputation, many described him as handsome, genial, and good-natured. Strangely enough, there were many stories of his kindness. From his hide-out, Lewis often descended on people in the Newville area. The three wealthiest residents were Mr. Sterrett, Mr. McKeehan and Captain Sharpe. Sterrett put his money into bonds, Sharpe into land, but McKeehan, an elderly gentleman, carried gold pieces. Lewis planned to waylay him as he rode home from church, carry him into the woods and tie him up until McKeehan revealed the hiding place of his treasure. However, Lewis confessed, "I did meet the old man one Sunday afternoon as he was returning home from church, but my heart failed me. I was struck by his benevolent countenance, his simplicity of manners. I could not touch him with the finger of violence." The McKeehan family regarded his escape as providential. Lewis reported, "I slept better than I had done for several nights before when the plan was being formulated."

Clyde Crouse's grandmother related another incident that took place in the town of Roxbury and confirmed Lewis' "Robin Hood" status. A poor townswoman, ill and unable to pay the doctor for his services, worried aloud about her difficulty. Hearing of it, Lewis relieved the good doctor of his cash one dark night and brought it to the woman so she could pay her debt.

Another story came from the area of the Seven Mountains. Rev. John Hutchinson was on his way to Bellefonte to preach for Rev. James Linn when he was held up by Lewis' gang and robbed of all his money and his watch. Hutchison said, "Now, men, I wish you would let me have fifty cents back; I am going to Bellefonte to preach, and I have not a cent to pay my way." Lewis asked, "Are you a minister?" When he affirmed that he was, Lewis said, "Give this man back his watch and money. We do not rob poor men nor ministers, for they are paid little enough." So Rev. Hutchison got his money and went on his way rejoicing.

David Lewis in his book, "The Confessions or Narrative on David Lewis" written in 1820, relates the final chapter of Lewis' life. Having robbed a wagon, Lewis and his fellow rogues were pursued. Connelly, part of the gang, was a violent vicious sort of man. When accosted, he opened fire. Lewis, on the other hand, avoided hitting anyone but was shot in the right arm in the ensuing gunfight. Taken prisoners, they were attended by three physicians and a minister. According to the account, "Lewis was tenderly removed to the jail at Bellefonte, but since he refused to allow his arm to be amputated, gangrene set in and he died on July 13, 1820, having finished his confession the day before." Lewis, as it was said, was a born leader among the criminal class.

Lewis and his gang were not the only ones who stole. A band of horse thieves drove animals from Virginia and Maryland through Path Valley and westward. According to oral history, Mrs. Alexander of Path Valley had a beautiful horse that she had returned to its stable after a lovely drive. The next morning, the horse was gone and never found until the next summer. A visitor to Ohio recognized the horse in a stable there. There wasn't any doubt of the horse's identity it was said. Meanwhile, towns were growing, more acres were being farmed, and new faces were appearing.

WAR OF 1812

CHAPTER SEVEN

*T*HE WAR OF 1812, sometimes called "President Madison's War," proved to be a testing point for the new nation. Opinions were sharply aired and loyalties were divided. The South and West favored war with Great Britain; New England and New York generally opposed it. Nevertheless, circumstances bearing on the United States slowly drew the young country into the conflict between England and France.

The high seas had become increasingly dangerous. British seamen, serving under harsh and difficult circumstances, sometimes deserted to serve on American ships. In turn, British officers often boarded American ships and pressed American sailors into service. According to one estimate, over six thousand American sailors suffered this fate.

Given these confrontations between American and British vessels, trade eventually suffered. American ships were continually on the seas as they transported textiles from New England, iron and glass from Pennsylvania, and agricultural products from the southern states. Fishing vessels plied the coasts. American vessels even sailed as far as Canton opening up trade with China.

Battle, when it came, would not only be fought on the high seas, but on the Great Lakes and adjacent areas that would eventually become metropolitan Detroit and Chicago. Control of interior lakes and rivers, such as the Mississippi, once again became points of conflict. People moving west encountered hostile Indians, some of them encouraged by the British to prey on settlers. These were skirmishes that preceded open hostilities.

Finally, on June 1, 1812, things came to a head. Impressment of seamen, interference with trade, the blockade of American ports, and the British encouragement of Indian aggression, prompted President Madison to ask Congress for a declaration of war against Great Britain. By the nineteenth, Congress voted for war, although the vote was far from unanimous.

Not unlike the minutemen of the Revolutionary War, the men of Path Valley observed the gathering war clouds and began to prepare. When war was officially declared, the Concord Light Infantry was ready to go. Thirty men under Captain Michael Harper and Major William McClellan departed in September, marching through Bedford, Pittsburgh, Meadville, and other points west. Around the middle of October, they marched to Buffalo where they remained until January when they were disbanded. A planned three-pronged invasion of Canada was drawn on paper but never realized.

In 1813, control of Lake Erie became an issue. During a battle in September, Captain Oliver Perry, who had quietly built a flotilla of ships called by some a "makeshift 10 vessel fleet," engaged the enemy in a bloody three-hour naval battle. During the battle, two natives from Juniata, Jacob Tool and Alexander Metlin came to the fore. When Perry's flag-ship, *Lawrence*, was sunk by the enemy, Perry was forced to transfer command to the *Niagara*. It was Tool and Metlin who rowed Commander Perry from his fast-sinking ship. Both were expert boatmen, having learned to handle oars on the ferry boats crossing the Juniata River at Mifflintown. Perry later reported to General William Harrison, "We have met the enemy, and they are ours." Oliver Perry and William Harrison eventually cleared the lakes of British forces.

During January 1814, Congress authorized raising an army of 62,773 men. The army at that time numbered around 11,000 and the assessment of army personnel was not positive. Many regular soldiers were described as the "offscourings of jails and pothouses." Senior officers, it was said, had "slunk into sloth or habits of intemperate drinking, and the new officers had for the most part been appointed for political reasons." The task of creating a strong military force was challenging.

Nevertheless, Path Valley forces were on duty and prepared to march. On February 16, Captain Samuel Dunn of lower Path Valley notified the members of his company of militia. "Take notice that you are hereby required personally, or by sufficient substitute, to appear at Loudon-Town properly armed and equipped for service at the hour of 12 o'clock noon, Tuesday the 1st of March as required. A Court Martial for the trial of delinquents (agreeably to the Laws of the United States) will sit at Loudon, on Wednesday the 2nd of March next." The company had already been drilling. Composed entirely of Scots-Irish, many were drawn from the iron works at Mt. Pleasant. They assembled at Loudon on March 1, 1814.

Unfortunately, they were without music to keep them in step while marching. At Everett, members raised money from their resources and purchased a violin. It was placed in the hands of Billy Woods, who it was said, "came as near to making a fiddle talk as any man who handled the bow." When the company marched through Pittsburgh, the spectators were much impressed as the soldiers kept step with the music of Billy's violin.

Joined by other troops, the company marched to Erie under Major William McClellan and there, having obtained muskets, they were placed in the fifth regiment of the Pennsylvania troops commanded by Colonel James Fenton. The entire army was placed under Major General Jacob Brown and participated in the Battles of Chippewa and Lundy's Lane, regarded by some as the most violent battles of the war. Wearily, they withdrew to Fort Erie. After setting a guard on British prisoners, they marched to what is now Albany, New York where they were mustered out. Sailing down the Hudson River, they landed at South Amboy in New Jersey and then marched to Fannettsburg, arriving on September 6, 1814. It was not until Saturday, October 8th that they received their pay.

The beloved company violin, which all had chipped in to buy, had to be fairly disposed of. It was decided that the violin should be awarded to the best marksman in the company. Captain Dunn, considered a "crack shot," excused himself. On the designated day, the contest began. The prize fell to Mr. John Walker who later became well known for his service in the Civil War. Eventually, Mr. Denny Walker, Esq., Walker's nephew, became the proud owner of the violin.

Meanwhile, American privateers captured a staggering 825 vessels off the coast of England! Morale was boosted when the American sloop of war, *Peacock,* captured a British brig carrying $120,000 in hard currency off the coast of Florida. The young nation was showing its strength.

During August 1814, the war came closer to home. With fewer than 5,000 men, the British landed near Washington, D.C., and met a slightly larger force of militia near Bladensburg. The militia fled before the British who set fire to the Capitol, the White House, some government buildings and private homes.

When a messenger from Washington arrived in Chambersburg with the news, bells were rung and drums and fifes called people to arms. Within hours, the news arrived in Path Valley. Captain Walker's notes reveal local response: "This was sufficient to stir up the feeling of patriotism to its utmost pitch. Those who had already made sacrifices for their country were not men to stand idly by while the…foreign foe invaded our soil, and the hand of vandals applied the torch." Plans were formed to march for Baltimore the next day, even though the next day was Sunday.

A lady, perhaps Ann Skinner Walker (1798-1881) described the scene on that "bright Sabbath morning" as she and other members of her family came across the mountain from Horse Valley to attend church. Crossing the Kittochtinny Mountain, they paused at the top, hearing to their surprise, martial music. Coming to the Conococheague Creek, they found a group of men gathering to march to the defense of Baltimore. It was a motley crew without uniforms and with only the arms they could gather together in haste.

Apparently, when word went out for men to gather for service, one man was out in his field working. His wife responded for him, saying that her husband could be counted on to join the group. As they turned to ride down the road, she called, "If he don't go, I will!" This group of men was one of seven companies from Franklin County. They arrived in time to defend Baltimore. Francis Scott Keye, seeing the flag still flying over Fort McHenry as it was bombarded, composed the "Star Spangled Banner."

During the fall of 1814, a fifty ship fleet with 7,500 veteran British soldiers aboard sailed for New Orleans, determined to take control of the Mississippi River. General Andrew Jackson was ready and waiting. Unknown to Jackson and his British opponent, the Treaty of Ghent ending the War of 1812, had been signed by peace commissioners from America, England, and France on December 14th. Strangely enough, the treaty did not address the issues that had caused the war, but focused on the release of prisoners, proposed adjustment of the Canadian border, and restoration of property among other things.

Meanwhile, the Battle of New Orleans was fiercely fought on January 8, 1815. In the half-hour battle, the British forces suffered 2,036 casualties. American casualties were dramatically lighter. Eight Americans were killed and thirteen wounded. Jackson's Tennessee and Kentucky sharpshooters had done their job from behind fortifications hastily constructed. This was the most spectacular victory of the war that had already ended. On February 17, 1815, the Senate ratified the Treaty of Ghent and President Madison announced the end of the war.

The War of 1812 strengthened national unity and bolstered a feeling of patriotism. Those who had settled farther west outside the boundaries of the original thirteen states now felt greater loyalty to the nation rather than the state. The nation had matured and was more cohesive, but there was still much work to be done.

The war pointed out the need for a well-trained army, banks, and some form of taxation to finance war, as well as roads and canals to transport produce and people. The future was filled with challenges.

THOSE WHO SERVED UNDER CAPTAIN SAMUEL DUNN

First Lieutenant– James McConnell
Second Lieutenant– Robert Foote
Third Lieutenant– John Favorite
Ensign– William Geddes
Sergeants– John Snively, Samuel Baker, John M. Shannon, James McHenry

Privates– Hugh Baker, Anthony Bates, Andrew Barclay, John Barclay, Jesse Beams, John Beatty, Levi Black, Frederick Boreaugh, John Brandt, John Brewster, George Bryon, William Buchanon, Barnabas Clark, James Compton, James Conner, Samuel Cramer, Thomas Cummings, John Cunningham, Samuel Davenport, Benjamin Davis, John Doyle, Robert Elder, James Elliot, Joseph Fingerty, Abraham Flagle, Jacob Frush, Jere Gift, Henry Halby, Nehemiah Harvey, Thomas Hays, Edward Heil, Hugh Henderson, Henry Hess, John Humbert, Robert Hunter, Enoch Johns, Robert Johnston, James Kirkwood, John Krotzer, Benjamin Long, David Leightner, Noah Mackey, Geroge Macomb, John Marshel, Samuel Mateer, John McConnell, Robert McConnell, William McClure, John McDowell, Absalom McIlwee, James McKein, Adam Meyers, John Miller, William Moore, John Murray, John Noble, Joseph Noble, John Over, Mathias Panther, Thomas Penwell, James Phipps, George Flucher, William Ransey, William Reed, Phillip Roan, Charles Runion, Peter Schell, William Sheets, John Shell, Barney Shipton, John Smith, Jacob Staley, Jacob Stevich, John Stewart, John Swanger, Samuel Swope, David Trindle, John Walker, William Williams, William Woods, Richard Wright, George Wrist, John Young, Robert Young, Jacob Zettle, John Stake

HARPER'S COMPANY FROM PATH VALLEY

Captain– Michael Harper

Lieutenant– William McKinzie

Ensign– John Campbell

Sergeants– William Irwin, James McKinzie, John Widney, Hugh Barrack

Corporals– Jeremiah Baker, Francis McCullogh, Samuel Campbell, James Girmeren

Privates– John Cannon, James Dever, Barnabas Donnelly, David Evans, Barnabas Fegan, Jere Hockenberry, James Hockenberry, George Irwin, James Linn, Samuel Phillips, Isaac Scooly, William Smith, Richard Scott, James Taylor, Peter Timmons

This group defended Baltimore when the British landed and burnt the capitol.

COMPANIES THAT LEFT THE COUNTY EARLY IN SEPTEMBER 1814

REGIMENT UNDER COLONEL JOHN FINDLAY

Captain– William Alexander
Lieutenant– Francis McConnell
Ensign– James Barkley
Sergeants– John Maclay, Richard Childerson, Peter Foreman, William Young
Corporal– John Sterrett

Privates– James Alexander, Thomas Childerstone, Edward Dunn, John Elder, Noah Elder, Andrew Foreman, William Finnerty, Thomas Geddis, John Harry, Samuel Hockenberry, John Hill, Thomas Harry, George Houston, James Irwin, James Jones, David Kyle, James McConnell, John Little, Robert Lewis, Robert McMillon, James McKibben, Robert McCleary, John McAllen, Joseph McKelvy, Hugh Maxwell, John McKee, John Neal, Peter Piper, John Patterson, John Ryan, William Shutter, Arthur Shields, John Vanlear, David Wallace, Peter Wilt

(Note: These names have been copied from old lists in original hand writing. Spellings are not always accurate.)

FANNETTSBURG, CARRICK FURNACE, BUNKER HILL (WILLOW HILL)

CHAPTER EIGHT

Fannettsburg was in the process of evolving into a village long before William McIntire began to sell lots for his "new town" in 1792. The Skinner Road brought endless traffic moving both east and west. The thud of hooves, the thunder of wagons, and human voices encouraging reluctant horses filled the air.

BUSINESSES

William Brewster, the first settler, operated a store at the top of the hill. He was soon joined by others along the Skinner Road whose businesses existed to serve the needs of teams and travelers. These included the following: William Boggs, a hatter; Robert Ramsey, saddler; and James Sweeny, postmaster and saddler. Patrick Collins, John Kyle, John McAllen, William McClay, George McCullich, H. S. McCune, George McKee, and John Witherow all owned establishments that probably served as inns near or along the Skinner Road.

By 1792, William McIntire arrived with his vision of a town planted on the hill and named after a place in County Donegal, Ireland. It was to be a center of commerce and prosperity. Lots for sale extended from the Conococheague Creek to within a few perches of the cross-road in the valley. (This road is now the current Route 75.) The sale was to take place on November 1, on a lot next to the home of William Brewster. According to records, only two lots were sold that day.

Over the next eight years, sixteen lots were sold. During that time, additional names and vocations are mentioned: James Culbertson, tanner; William Davison, blacksmith; Patrick Collins, John Kyle and Robert Newel, merchants; John Huston, Theopholis Cissna, and William Piper, innkeepers.

By 1825, sixty-seven lots had been sold and we find numerous new vocations listed: John Witherow, carpenter; John Walker, tanner; John Campbell, cabinet-maker and wheelwright; William Boggs, hatter; Edward Connell, blacksmith; Samuel Land, tailor; John Noble, pump maker; Edward Thompson, weaver; Robert Ransey, saddler; William Maclay, innkeeper; William Anderson, tanner; Thomas Campbell, hatter; David Fletcher and William Dunkle, wagon makers; John Davison and Joseph Martin, black-smiths. Eventually, a broom factory, a cigar-making establishment, whip factories, and creameries were established. John Skinner and John McAllen, who arrived sometime during 1787, established brick kilns in the area. Four men owned six stills between them. As time passed, William McClay, John Rotz, Robert McMallan, and James Elliott opened tanneries. Fannettsburg was growing and becoming the center of commerce in the southern end of Path Valley. McIntire's dream was materializing.

Many of the old structures built in the early days of Fannettsburg are still standing. Some have been beautifully restored, while others wait for the hand of those who have vision and appreciate the value of historical preservation.

At the eastern end of town is a beautiful brick structure identified as the McAllen Inn. Tradition claims that George Washington made a brief stop here while passing through town. Within are remnants of a colonial bar, a small room to provide lodging for a prisoner and sheriff, and large rooms to accommodate guests. In old diaries, people mention their stay at the inn in positive terms. The brick house adjacent to the inn was built to house the help required to serve the patrons. John McAllen bought large tracts of land and built brick kilns which furnished materials to construct a number of homes. He also erected four mills—two sawmills and two flouring mills.

John F. McAllen, Esquire, another member of the family, published the area's first newspaper, the *Path Valley News*. He also kept a small store at that end of town "so people would not have to climb the Hill!"

At the western end of town stands a beautiful stone structure bearing the date 1842 and the name Kegerreis. Once home of the Noble family, it is now owned by Doris and Sam Crider. An earlier part of the structure served as a hostel for drovers. It was a lovely stopping place before ascending the dreaded Tuscarora Mountain and undoubtedly rang with lively music and stories of wild adventure.

North of Fannettsburg stands another important stone house built by John and Mary Skinner from England and treasured in their family for generations. The last owner in the family was Mary Skinner who taught school in the valley for many years. The Park home, the Walker farm, the many others are all prime examples of historically valuable and beautifully proportioned homes.

MILLS

Old-timers describe an era when boots were necessary to cope with perpetually moist land, plentiful water, and creeks that ran high. Early settlers capitalized on the water power available along many creeks. In the Fannettsburg area, the creeks were dotted with mills and the air filled with the low hum of the water wheels and the grinding of mill stones. Mills were built to saw wood and grind corn, wheat, rye and oats into flour for pancakes, corn pone and bread, essentials in the diet of that day. In some areas, there were weaving and fulling mills, woolen and powder mills.

Around 1775, James McCurdy built a grist mill on the west branch of the Conocoheague Creek near Willow Hill. It was in operation until after 1909 when John Kuhn owned it. The Stake mill at Willow Hill and the Philip Hammond mill took their power from the same stream. The west branch of the Conococheague supplied Mr. Alexander's mill and one owned by Mr. Van Scyoc in Amberson. The profusion of mills included those owned by the Copely family, Richard Childerson, Cutlip Everett, John McVitty, the Shields family, Nicholas Patterson, and George Taylor. As the years passed, Samuel Dunn, James Philips, John Karey, and John McAllen were added to the list of mill owners.

The Hoover mill, which remained in family hands for many years, still stands as an informal memorial to the mills of Path Valley and their rich history. Even after the Hoover mill, painted red and yellow, was closed, the cheese wheel and hanging apron remained in place, as if anticipating a future. The mill was so loved by Mr. Hoover that he decreed his funeral procession must pass by it in a final farewell.

It was said that mills made their own music. The rhythmic sloshing of the waterwheel may have sounded soothing and peaceful, but when the mill started up, "the weight of the water seemed to create a giant shudder," according to one mill owner. "Huge oak beams quivered as the heavy wooden gears squeaked, and the whole building seemed to strain as the wheel began to turn." As another miller explained, "There was a special and overwhelming awareness of power that makes you feel a part of the machine and the machine a part of you." Perhaps, this explains the close relationship Mr. Hoover had with his mill.

To build and repair the machinery of the mills required the services of trained and skilled workmen known as millwrights, an indispensable group of men who quietly kept the production lines moving. As early as 1792, millstones were made in Chambersburg by James Falkner, Jr.

These mills were gathering places for those who came to have the harvest of their fields ground into flour. At the mill, people shared common concerns and exchanged information, political views, and stories. In that sense, the mills not only sustained bodies but also spirits as they served as centers of communication.

The growth of towns and small businesses depended on the produce of the farms. During these years, farmers were still clearing land, planting, scything, and threshing, all without modern machinery. As the town grew, so did the needs of a growing population. With an eye to the future, William McIntire planted the first orchard.

SCHOOLS

With growing pains and large families came an urgent need for schools. Parents felt strongly that their children must be educated in order to read Scripture, their first priority, and after that to enhance their knowledge and to learn enough to carry on the family business. It was said that where there were Presbyterians, there were subscription (or private) schools.

The first school house was a log building erected sometime before 1792 on land owned by William McIntire north of Fannettsburg and across the road from the Reformed Church. According to some records, it was already in session the year Fannettsburg was laid out. The school was of simple construction with a clapboard roof and puncheon floor. Light filtered in between the logs which were not caulked. In the wind and snow of winter, these spaces were covered with greased paper. Students attended school six days a week, learning to read, write and cipher (arithmetic). One can imagine the low murmur of voices and the scratching of quill pens.

The school curriculum in those early years was closely connected to Christianity. In the spring, children were required to recite the Westminster Shorter Catechism (107 questions) and were examined by Rev. Amos McGinley. As members of the church, teens and adults were required to memorize the Westminster Larger Catechism (196 questions) and were thoroughly examined. It was assumed church members had a thorough knowledge of Scripture and some understanding of Presbyterian theology. Upon occasion, Rev. McGinley handed out a list of Bible questions from the pulpit and informed the recipients they had several weeks to prepare.

Answers were to be written out and presented on specified days. Standing before their wives and children, some men approached the challenge with confidence, but others were nervous and embarrassed, particularly if their reading skills were wanting. Sometimes arguments broke out over interpretation, and it was Rev. McGinley's task to settle the issue with tact. In an effort to support their position, many returned to their study of Scripture. Education took place on many different levels in the community and continued throughout life.

Teachers in these early schools were generally farmer's sons who possessed both curiosity and a desire to continue their own education. Many had acquired some measure of formal education before taking up the vocation. Some excelled in writing as evidenced by the contents of old documents.

Teachers in subscription schools boarded with the families of their students and were often itinerants. For many youngsters having a teacher stay with them was a special privilege. Families made an effort to serve the teacher's favorite foods, particularly if the teacher was well liked. In this way, teachers became acquainted with the parents and homes of their students which was to their advantage.

Discipline was strict both at home and at school. The rod or cat-o'-nine-tails (Master William Mackey's favorite) was applied liberally. Master Wightman made the boys bite on the end of a broomstick or two boys were required to stand back to back and support a stick of wood between them. Less often, a boy was required to sit between two girls with a bonnet on his head, a punishment sometimes more difficult for the girls than the offender. The least of all punishments was to walk the length of a crack in the floor. In the records of those days, all forms of punishment mention boys rather than girls.

The last teacher in the subscription school was William A. Mackey who became the first to teach in the public school. Other teachers were Master Morrow who taught for many years; Master Sturgis; Master James Peoples described as a witty and eccentric Irishman; Thomas Snodgrass, Leander Karr, Robert Karr, John Lack, and John Brewster.

The Common School opened in 1834. Unlike many who were reluctant to assume the expenses of public education, five Path Valley men rode to the state capital where the subject was under debate, and declared their solid support for public schools. The public school offered an elementary grade education and opened on January 1, 1835. Fannett Township received $64 from the state; the total amount spent was $194.70.

The job description of Thomas Doyle who was hired to teach school in Amberson Valley on September 24, 1838, gives us an insight into the regiment and curriculum of the day. They were required to teach eight hours a day, twenty-six days a month. At the end of the month, Thomas was evaluated by the directors. The curriculum included reading, writing, and arithmetic. School books included a spelling book, an English reader, a New Testament, and a simple arithmetic text. Later a manual of United States history, a grammar book and geography book were added. The teacher was paid $15 a month and instructed to keep, "a regular school both as to time and morals."

Eventually, enrollment reached between seventy-five and ninety pupils and required more room. A new log school was built at the other end of town. In 1823, a large stone schoolhouse was built, but it burned down in 1864. Other schools were built in outlying areas near homes: Center, Stoney Point Road, Metal, and near the Flickinger and Brown homes.

CHURCHES

While education was considered important, it was the church that sustained the courage and vision to see this small area of God's earth as a kingdom where His will would be accomplished. This belief was a core value for these early Presbyterians.

By 1794, the Presbyterians had not only called Rev. David Denny who would share his pastoral services with Upper Path Valley Presbyterian Church, preaching on alternate Sundays, but they had built a second church building in a grove of handsome oaks near a spring. Here, people gathered between services to enjoy the cold water and breezes.

Winter weather brought other challenges. Rev. Amos McGinley who followed Rev. Denny wrote, "Many a ludicrous thought has started in the mind of your speaker as he looked out from the little tub pulpit over his congregation with forms drawn up, shivering, agitated, and puffing away like so many little stationary engines; stationary from a sense of duty but eager to hear the 'Amen' that they might be off to their comfortable houses." Elders who were ordained before 1800 were: David Walker, Judge William McClay, Paul Giddis, and John Campbell.

In 1832, a third church, larger and more comfortable, was built. It was called the "White Church." S. S. Wylie recorded that the church had "two entrances from the west side facing the road and an entrance from the north and south, the latter with large stone steps. The old-fashioned dark mahogany pulpit was high, mounted by way of a winding stairway on either side. Large red curtains covered the entire wall back of the pulpit." Two large ten-plate stoves, connected with pipes to a large drum overhead, heated the building in winter which was a great comfort to the congregation.

The church-goers' garb has been described by Fred Shearer in his publication. The ladies wore woolen flannel dresses, specially saved for the occasion. Making the dresses meant carding, spinning, and weaving the wool before finally cutting and sewing the garment, all by hand. Women's calfskin shoes were made at home of tanned leather. The services of a shoemaker were sometimes required.

The men wore buckskin breeches, blacked and buffed every week for Sunday service. Blue yarn knit stockings covered their legs to the knee, and some shoes featured brass buckles, often handed down from one generation to another. They wore white shirts, carefully cared for to wear the next Sunday.

The Presbyterian churches in the valley continued to flourish. When Rev. Denny resigned, Rev. McGinley was called to serve both Upper and Lower Path Valley Presbyterian churches. Ordained by Carlisle Presbytery at Greencastle, McGinley was installed on June 19, 1803. Every fourth Sunday, he rode across the mountain on an old trail and preached a sermon in Aughwich

Valley, Burnt Cabins and at the Cree schoolhouse near Decorum. The Burnt Cabins Presbyterian Church was dedicated on Christmas Day, 1851.

A large muscular man, McGinley was imposing in the pulpit. Preaching for the most part extemporaneously, he delivered sermons described as "sound, practical and imaginative." He was remembered for his habit of drawing a large silk handkerchief through his hand numerous times during the service, apparently to relieve stress. A kindly man, he "drew young people to him like a magnet."

Known for his gifts as a counselor, McGinley settled many disputes. Some believed he had some inner instinct that led him to scenes of conflict. He often appeared unexpectedly to mediate differences.

In 1820, a minister from the Church of England visited Amberson and decided to organize a new church there. Although he managed to build a church, he met many obstacles as he struggled to organize the congregation. Rev. McGinley was not about to allow a portion of his congregation to be lured away and viewed his rival as a man "out of order" in both spirit and understanding, and faulted his views on doctrine and theology. Applying pressure in this way, McGinley discouraged the newcomer who soon left looking for a more fertile field.

Although membership in the Lower Path Valley Church rose and in 1831 accepted 127 new members, there was a continual exodus of the area's people who were drawn to cheap land farther west. In spite of these losses, membership continued to climb. During his pastorate, Reverend McGinley married 697 couples.

Known for his punctuality, Rev. McGinley managed to arrive at his destination on time, regardless of weather or other obstacles. Later, when his wife's mode of travel changed from sidesaddle to carriage, McGinley continued to leave early on horseback.

Although his salary was never in excess of $400 a year, by 1847 Rev. McGinley managed to acquire sixty acres of land, twelve acres of meadow, two horses, three cows, and a carriage. He was a wise manager of his resources. Rev. and Mrs. McGinley's three children all married people in the valley.

In 1829, John married Eliza McCormick, E.J. McGinley married Dr. J. K. McCurdy, and Sarah married Samuel Walker.

Rev. McGinley died on May 1, 1856. His final resting place was the Lower Path Valley Presbyterian cemetery. Elders who served during his ministry were Daniel Brown, Joseph Brown, James Campbell, John Campbell, James Cree, Sr., James Cree, Jr., George Elliott, William Elliott, Paul Geddes, William McClay, Alexander Walker, David Walker, and James Walker. The Rev. L. W. Williams was called to the Lower Path Valley Presbyterian Church in 1851, but was not installed until 1853. By 1855, he had moved on.

During this first half of the century, other churches were organized, one of them the Methodist church in 1837. According to some records, John Noble, Sr. donated the land and in partnership with George Dunkle built the church supplying materials and labor. For a short period of time, members met in the schoolhouse. The congregation included the Donathens, Everetts, Geyers, Runks, Stewarts, Lessigs, Glasses, Jones' and Traxlers.

The German Reformed Church north of Fannettsburg was erected in 1840 on a lot purchased from Henry and Sarah Nusbaum for five dollars. A lovely stone building, it originally had two doors opening to the sanctuary, one for men and the other for women. Rev. Jacob Shade was the first minister, Henry Wineman, Sr. and George Umbrell the first elders, and George Fierling the first deacon. In addition to the officers, other early members were T. Barclay, Melchior Conrad, Mary Farling, Barbara Flickinger, Mary A. Kegerries, Jacob Kegerries, Evan Miller, Martha Philips, Rehanna Philips, Abram Rosenberry, John Stewart, Matthew Umbrell, Catherine Walker, Henry Walker and Elizabeth Wood.

A story passed down orally concerns an important day in the Reformed Church. Holy Communion was to be celebrated. Everyone waited patiently to receive the bread and drink wine from the common cup which was a large, ornate chalice. Suddenly, there was a lengthy pause. A flustered female member and the pastor were seen peering into the chalice. Then the service resumed. When worship ended and the congregation dismissed, the inquisitive young man decided to peer into the room through an open window.

Looking inside the church, he saw the minister and church member probing through the deep purple wine in the bottom of the chalice. With a look of triumph, the minister triumphantly pulled forth a set of artificial teeth. The worshiper hurriedly placed them in her mouth and hurried from the church. Stifled laughter erupted from the onlooker who entered the story in the annals of history.

COMMUNITY LIFE

Fannettsburg was always a lively place. It was said by some that the town was "churned up" by the devil himself, who had created the town's hill by dumping a load of slate and stones on it. A group of men playing "devil cards" in the Walker house one night were said to have heard the rattling of chains and the smell brimstone as the devil came back to check on his work.

The town was not always tranquil. Sometimes tempers flared. One newspaper article reported, "Last Monday morning we had quite a serious shooting affray in our quiet little village in which Dr. R. Alexander was seriously wounded by R. E. Typer. Dr. Alexander, hearing that Typer had some ill feelings toward him, went to the P.O. to talk with him. Just as he entered the door, Typer took aim at him with a revolver, the ball taking effect in the breast. Dr. Alexander knowing his only chance for life was to run, started for Weinman Brother's Store. Typer followed him, firing two shots at him on the way, following him into the store, firing more shots. One ball struck Mr. Henry Weinman on the shoulder, fortunately, not wounding him. The other struck Dr. Alexander in the head entering just back of the ear and passing along the skull bone, coming out just over the eye. Typer was arrested and taken to jail. We are glad to state that the Doctor is recovering slowly, but not out of danger. Dr. A. is one of our best citizens and Mr. Typer postmaster of this place."

Tempers got out of hand at times! Mr. Walker kept order in his store by strongly suggesting when men got too vociferous, they go home and come back the next evening. At times, informal groups served as moral guides. For example, some men indulged themselves by buying a nickel's worth of cheese and three cents' worth of crackers out of the barrel behind the counter. Other men expressed their disapproval by asking, "What about the women and children at home?" They are missing the treat!"

In spite of their differences, whether great or small, most citizens looked out for one another. Allen Mort, the town constable, was known as a "fine gentleman in both appearance and kindly approach to any problem." His first case involved the Kiner family who were "to be sold out" for debt. The creditors were waiting to take everything – chairs, beds, table, and sewing machine. Mrs. Kiner and the children stood crying. Her husband mournfully asked Mr. Mort, "What am I to do?" All Allen Mort had was forty dollars, but with it he paid the debt and saved the family. Asked to explain, his answer was, "What would any Christian do?"

CARRICK FURNACE

Meanwhile, farther south in the valley, clouds reflected the reddish glow of the first iron furnace, named Mt. Pleasant. It had a long and interesting history. The iron industry was started in 1783 by William and George Chambers, who built the first furnace, which was later owned and operated by Thomas Lindsay Dunn. The furnace eventually ran into difficulties. The water supply was uncertain. A dam and a second furnace were built, but high water caused a collapse of the whole system. To compound difficulties, the supply of charcoal was almost exhausted. Dunn who married Elizabeth Holliday in the late 1780's, died at Mount Pleasant in 1816 and was buried in the Lower Path Valley Presbyterian cemetery.

When Samuel Dunn inherited the Mt. Pleasant furnace from his father, he had two partners: Thomas McCullock, Esq. who handled legal matters, and James Bard who was not only a metallurgist but possessed great foresight and energy. Samuel had acquired some scientific knowledge of iron production while studying at Dickinson College.

When the future of Mt. Pleasant came into question, James Bard discovered what he thought was a much larger and superior deposit of iron ore and limestone. The iron ore ran along the base of Tuscarora Mountain from Richmond to Spring Run and was found on farms owned by William Johnson, T. W. McAllen, and George Wineman. The proposed site also caught the wind which meant there would be a much needed draft for efficient fuel consumption. Water was available from the dam at the gristmill. Eventually, the decision was made to build a furnace located midway between Mt. Pleasant and Fannettsburg named Carrick. Work began immediately to erect the furnace, forge, bellows-house, blacksmith shop, and install the necessary equipment which cost $3,500.

People living in the area around Fannettsburg could often see the glow of the furnace reflected in the night sky. From time to time sparks scattered above the forests like fireworks in the darkness. Noise emanated from the forge where pig iron was made into bars of wrought iron. There was an irregular splash of falling water from the wheel of the mill where flour and meal were produced to supply the community's needs. A sawmill ran regularly to supply lumber to build company houses and repair wagons. All these sights and sounds were part of life around the Carrick Furnace.

The community was large and closely knit. Between twenty and thirty houses were built for employees and their families. Foundrymen and other skilled workers filled four boarding houses. Colliers lived in cabins scattered throughout the area. The Mansion House, where the owner lived, was large enough to accommodate parties and dances, the latter accompanied by the sound of fiddles. There were cornhusking gatherings, barn dances, and quilting and skating parties. Life was far from dull for anyone. The children of miners and colliers mingled and played with the children of bosses and the owner. No one was excluded. People looking at the community from outside found something to envy.

According to the company payroll records, around 200 workers were required to run the operation. The actual process of producing iron required 20. Ten were used each shift which changed at 11:00 a.m. and 11:00 p.m. at which time castings were usually made. Two "fillers" on each shift stood at the top of the furnace and fed the cupola at specified times as instructed by foundrymen supervising the process. First came the coal, then iron ore, limestone, and finally charcoal. The "gutterman" made the sandy forms for castings which collected molten iron. The process required not only knowledge and experience, but awareness and care.

A considerable labor force supplied the materials for production. Charcoal, for example, required acres of timberland. The company owned 7,000 acres of land in Letterkenny, Metal, and Peters townships in Franklin County and additional land elsewhere. The amount of wood required to produce charcoal was tremendous. One acre of good timber could produce only seventy-five cords of wood, and twenty-five to fifty cords were required for one burning. The operation required tremendous labor and resources. Furthermore, after a cutting, the landscape remained scalped and barren for many years. Finally, the expense of hauling wood from a distance contributed to the demise of the iron industry.

During this period of time, however, the company flourished and Carrick products were in demand. The ten-plate Carrick stoves built in William Nunan's small foundry were in great demand. Each bore the stamp, "Samuel Dunn and Co.," affirming their authenticity. The company also made cast-iron pipe for the Fort Loudon Water Company in the late 1830's. Hinges, locks, iron cooking pots, fireplace inserts, and other small items also bore their name.

The financial panic of 1837 proved fatal to the company, however. It was sold in the fall of 1843 and conveyed to the Bank of Chambersburg. The sparks and glare of the furnace in the night sky were seen no more. Silence returned to the Tuscarora Path and company houses fell into disrepair. Another chapter closed.

Meanwhile, schools, churches, homes, and businesses continued to flourish as the valley's population grew. Fannettsburg was becoming a strong community and commercial center in the southern end of Path Valley, and Concord was growing in the north. In the future, people of both would work together to create a unit important to the growth of our young nation.

BUNKER HILL

A short distance north of Fannettsburg, there was a small settlement called Bunker Hill after the significant battle in the Revolution. As early as 1827, a military review was organized. The parade took place in the fields owned by George Shearer in an area in front of A.M. Walker's property and a lot owned by John Wolf. Anthony Klippinger's hotel enjoyed a good business as officers and others celebrated around the dinner tables. The event drew great crowds from miles around.

Major James McCurdy and his wife moved to Bunker Hill from their farm in 1838 and McCurdy opened a blacksmith shop near their home in 1840. Mary B. McCurdy taught at Centre School and was described as "one of the best teachers in Metal Township."

In 1878, the post office was established and the village renamed Willow Hill. Mr. Charles Fleming was the first postmaster and also established a small store. In time, other people moved to town, among them J. F. Crouse, Jacob Klippinger, Lavinia Flickinger, and J. B. Alexander.

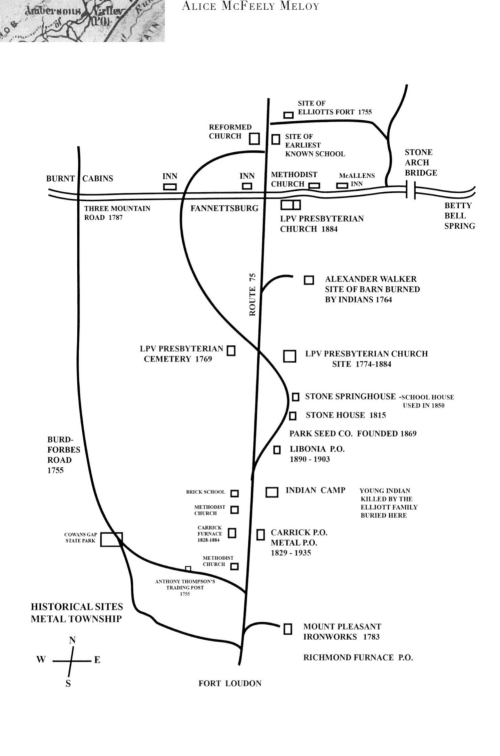

Map of early Fannettsburg.

The stone arch bridge east of Fannettsburg was
built by John Skinner and son.

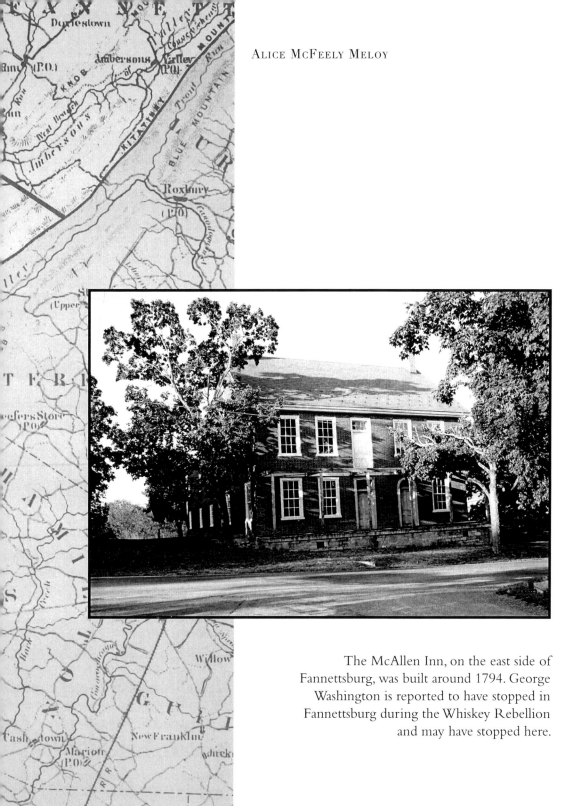

The McAllen Inn, on the east side of Fannettsburg, was built around 1794. George Washington is reported to have stopped in Fannettsburg during the Whiskey Rebellion and may have stopped here.

The Hoover Mill on Creek Road
between Fannettsburg and Willow Hill.

Crosskeys Inn, west of Fannettsburg, was
built in 1842 by the Keggereis family to house
cattle drovers.

The Skinner House, located just north of Fannettsburg, was one of the earliest in the area.

CONCORD

CHAPTER NINE

AFTER THE REVOLUTION, wagons carrying settlers came rolling over the Tuscarora Path, not only from Fort Loudon in the south, but through the Concord Narrows in the north. Some traveled the Juniata River on rafts from Harrisburg and settled along the Tuscarora Path in the area north of Path Valley. Drawn by friends or family, some made it through the most hazardous part of the journey – the stony, treacherous gap into what became Concord.

James Widney, a man of substance, was one of the first settlers. He bought 600 acres from the Coulters in 1784 and dreamed of creating a town. There was water in abundance, and in time, with the improvement of roads, the area had the potential to become a center of commerce serving several valleys.

Friends and families back in Ireland struggled with the decision to follow. As reported in the Linn family history, "Many and earnest were the conferences held by the Widney's, Linn's, and Irvine's concerning the wisdom of leaving home and kindred to live where the war whoop of the savage was heard and the smoke of cabins burned by the hand of the red man was daily rising." By this time, however, the Indians who remained in the area lived peacefully alongside their white neighbors. Finally, in 1788, the Linn family made the decision to join the Widneys in the New World. Farewells were said and tears shed as they boarded the ship at Londonderry and watched the Emerald Isle disappear from sight.

Weeks later, their ship docked at Philadelphia, known as an important city of the Western world even then. After viewing Independence Hall, symbol of the nation's freedom, the Linns made the necessary purchases to prepare for the journey. Better endowed than most, they started west by wagon stocked with provisions and household goods, destination Lancaster, then Fort Loudon. From there, it was still a long and difficult trip to the Widney's. One can only imagine the sense of relief when they finally arrived at the Widney's hillside home with its view of the valley.

One by one, families followed. Many of them bought land from James Widney. Laying out lots in a town named after Concord, Massachusetts, where the early battle for freedom had been fought, the town began to take shape.

Many who came over left behind a proud history. James Widney had inherited his family's ancestral estate but sold it to come to America. William Erwin had been a secretary and adjutant to King Robert the Bruce of Scotland and had built a castle in Ireland. The Harris family had received an estate in return for their service in the Battle of Hastings in 1098. Catherine Robertson was a direct descendent of the Campbells of Inverary Castle in Argyle, Scotland. Many other settlers were also descendants of well-known families.

Before the turn of the century, the area had been settled by the Pomeroy, Skinner, Widney, Harris, Erwin, Linn, Wallace, McElheny, McKenzie, McMullan (spelled numerous ways), Little, Crawford, Hockenberry, Ferguson, Robertson, Wilson, Campbell, Loughridge, Murray, Maxwell, McClure, and Doyle families. Three traits distinguished these Scots-Irish: a passionate faith, a zeal for education, and a love of freedom.

Churches

Many of these early settlers were United Presbyterians, formerly known as Seceders or Associate Reformed. There were differences between these Presbyterians and those who founded the Upper and Lower Path Valley Presbyterian churches. In the United Presbyterian Church, slavery was considered a moral evil and slave owners were not accepted as church members. Neither were members associated with secret orders nor those who voted for anyone who subscribed to the Constitution without first subscribing to the supremacy of God. Later, the differences between the United Presbyterians and the Presbyterians faded until finally they merged in the 20th century. Even in the early days, however, one family was known to attend both the United Presbyterian Church in Concord and the Presbyterian Church in Spring Run.

Some of these Presbyterians had been elders in their native land. Undoubtedly, with the dream of founding a kirk (church), they took responsibility for gathering others for prayer and Bible reading before being organized into a congregation by an official from their denomination. In these early days, responsibility for worship was often left in the hands of elders. The first elders of the United Presbyterian Church were David Ferguson, James Wilson, and James Little. Core members included Dr. Samuel Crawford, William Harris, Squire Orr, Squire Glenn, William Erwin, George Johnston, William Robertson, and the Campbell family.

Served by itinerant preachers on an irregular basis, it was 1815 before a stone church was built on the crest of the southern hill above Concord, a building not noted for its comfort or its attractiveness. The pews, benches without backs, filled half the sanctuary. The pulpit was "large, high, and unsightly." If the minister was short, he could barely be seen. Undoubtedly, its location on the crest of the hill made it susceptible to the cold winds of winter and the heat of summer.

The Campbell family walked to church, following a trail over the mountain from what is now Perry County. The Robertsons walked around the edge of the Round Top from Burns Valley and followed the trail into Concord. Many worshipers were weary even before settling on the hard benches for a two-or three-hour sermon. During this time, babies and small children were expected to remain silent.

Sermons were designed (in both length and intensity) to provide spiritual nourishment for many weeks at a time. Clergy traveled great distances and preached to churches scattered over a large area. Worship every Sunday would be a future luxury when a full-time preacher could be called. Psalms were the only acceptable hymn forms and were sung without musical accompaniment. A leader "lined" out the tune by singing a phrase the worshipers repeated. Prayers, often half an hour in length, were offered as the congregation stood in respect and devotion. At noon, there was a break and someone was sent to the spring above the church for water. Picnic baskets were brought out for a period of socializing until the afternoon service began.

When a permanent minister was called, regular services began. One of the most important was the celebration of the Lord's Supper. Communion was taken very seriously. Before one took his or her place at the table in front of the church to receive the elements, there was a week of preaching and ministers would urge their flocks to examine their lives. Elders and ministers often visited church members to question them on their understanding of right doctrine and to examine the moral state of their lives. If satisfied, the church member was given a small metal token that would admit him or her to the communion table. If not, amends had to be made to rectify the matter. Worship, repentance and prayer prepared them to come to the Lord's Table – a high and holy moment for most. Some women had a black taffeta or satin dress that they wore only on these occasions. In some areas, the service was followed by a Monday service of thanksgiving. The homes of Presbyterians in Concord were filled with guests from outlying areas, some traveling for miles to celebrate communion.

The Sabbath was kept holy and quiet. Cooking was not allowed. One faithful church member was informed during the service that the minister was coming for dinner at her home. Although it would be a cold dinner for cooking was forbidden, nevertheless she suddenly remembered that coffee had not been ground the preceding day. In an act of desperation, this good

Presbyterian sent the hired help to the barn to grind coffee needed for the guest, as if this offensive act could not be observed by God.

The Sabbath was also a day of quiet rest. Children were not allowed to play their usual rough-and-tumble games, but were required to sit quietly and either read or listen to Bible stories. Some were fortunate enough to own a small replica of Noah's Ark and animals which provided some acceptable playtime. One thoughtless father sent his young daughter to call the sheep in from pasture. Creating noise on the Sabbath was deemed a sin. She stood on the hill summoning her courage. Taking a deep breath, she called, and lived to tell the tale. Although it seems irrational today, the old strictures were solid reminders that God was to be honored and a day of rest was one of his gifts.

Ministers connected with the United Presbyterian Church were Rev. James Browne, Rev. Alexander McCahon, and in 1836 Dr. Sharp of Newville. When Concord was yoked with Chambersburg, Rev. Robert Gracey of Big Spring served. According to Presbytery minutes, his ministry of fifteen years was exemplary and influential. Many church members mourned their loss when he moved to Pittsburgh. Finally, the Concord United Presbyterian Church developed a relationship with the Tuscarora United Presbyterian Church and was served by Rev. Magill. The stone church was no longer in use by 1850. In the 1860s, the United Presbyterians built a new brick church which still stands today.

At the same time the Presbyterian Church was organizing, the Widney and Linn families became a formidable force for founding Methodism in Concord. It was said of the Widneys that they were great readers and not afraid of controversy. Strong opponents of the Presbyterian doctrine of double predestination, wherein it was believed that some were foreordained to be saved, but others judged and doomed, they believed in John Wesley's doctrine of grace and grace alone. (Presbyterian doctrine was later changed.)

James Wilson who became the postmaster was an ardent Presbyterian. James Widney, while a close friend, violently opposed the doctrine of double predestination. They frequently argued, and could be heard shouting important passages from various writings of Calvin and Wesley. When such encounters took place in the post office, neighbors stopped to listen.

The pitch and volume of the Scottish brogue increased until the walls seemed to shake. Wilson frequently won the argument, but Widney went home and put his arguments on paper in an effort to destroy Wilson's good Presbyterian logic, preparing himself for the next round of battle. To their credit, they remained good friends.

Widney, a native of the County of Armagh in Northern Ireland, had known John Wesley in Ireland and had served as a Methodist class leader. Now, however, these newly arrived Methodists were without preaching or organization. It was 1784 before the Methodist Episcopal Church of America was established in Baltimore. At that time, Francis Asbury was a consecrated bishop. Known as a "pastor to pastors and a shepherd to the people," he began visits to the field to learn about the people and their needs. In his journal he wrote, "I feel and have felt for thirty-two years, for Pennsylvania the most wealthy and the most careless about God and the things of God... I hope God will save the state and the churches."

Asbury's travels on horseback over heavily wooded mountains were not easy, and he was not an expert rider. Traveling on a mare rather than a high-spirited stallion, his gray-garbed figure and broad-brimmed hat became a familiar sight in central Pennsylvania. Attentive and observant, he sometimes broke new trails and found people who had been overlooked. For this reason, he found himself in Concord after a rather unsuccessful preaching mission in Carlisle.

Asbury spent several days in the homes of two or three families in the area. The worship service took place in a large log cabin called, "Castle Cool," which stood on the crest of the hill east of the diamond. Upon departing, Asbury urged James Widney to call his neighbors together every Sunday, to pray with them and to instruct them on the way to heaven.

After Asbury's visit, lay reading and preaching were established and invitations sent out far and wide. It was said of the recipients that "when they were assured of the deep religious enthusiasm and fervid zeal of their host, they needed no second invitation." It has been reported that James Widney had a horn that echoed throughout the hills and into the valley, calling people to worship. The number of people responding rapidly increased. Some called the cabin where they met, "Immanuel, God with Us."

The first Methodist Society was formed with eleven charter members, including Hugh Linn, his wife and their three children, John, Mary, and Hugh, Jr. A complete list of names has not been found, but we can assume that the Widney and Linn families accounted for many of the original eleven. James Widney was appointed the first class leader. As time passed, Hugh Linn and Robert McClay earned the nicknames, Caleb and Joshua, Old Testament figures who led the Israelites to the Promised Land.

As the Concord Methodists grew in number, a log structure was built on land belonging to James Widney. In 1803, he conveyed it to the trustees: James Campbell, Robert Maclay, Charles Widney, John Hockenberry, and John Widney. The land lay south of town where the Methodist cemetery is now located. As the founding document stated, "It was to be a place of worship…to be held by them forever." The site of the log church was near the Pomeroy lot.

In the early 1800's, a controversy arose within the Methodist Episcopal churches on the matter of representation to the annual conference. At the time, the churches were represented only by ministers who therefore controlled the laws and direction of the church. A group contended, time after time, that lay representation was needed. Their petition was rejected repeatedly until a convention was held in Baltimore. There the Methodist Protestant Church was born and included both ministers and lay representation. This explains the reason for two Methodist churches in Concord, one a Methodist Episcopal, the other Methodist Protestant.

Amid continuing controversy, a Methodist Protestant Church was built on the western side of the Tuscarora Creek, south of the bridge in a grove of mammoth pine trees. A lovely yellow plaster church, it was the first Methodist Protestant Church in the valley. After a period of time, controversy died and members who for the most part lived in the Doylesburg area, decided to relocate. The yellow church in the pines sat vacant and years later fell into disuse and finally in ruins. According to some, Concord had become "over-churched."

Side by side, the United Presbyterians and Methodists grew in numbers and in faith. They served the community well and from this small town and valley their commitment took them to the far corners of the world.

Robert Maclay, whose tomb is located on the exact spot where the pulpit of the first log church stood, had five sons and four daughters. The oldest daughter, Eleanor, married Joseph Pomeroy in 1826 and was said to be "uncommonly brilliant." She could repeat chapter after chapter of the Bible with ease.

Eleanor's brothers, John, Charles, Alexander, Robert, and William entered the Methodist ministry and carried the gospel across the country and around the world. John replaced William Turner, called the "Father of Hawaiian Methodism," and helped secure the Methodist Church in what would become our fiftieth state. Charles served the California Missionary Conference until his health suffered. Eventually, he gave $150,000 to establish the Maclay College of Theology, now known as the School of Theology at Claremont. Alexander became a supply pastor for the California Conference and brought the gospel to mining camps on the frontier. William became a professor at California Wesleyan University, and shortly afterward a college president, an elder, and a California legislator.

It was Robert Maclay, however, who left the Gettysburg circuit to go as a missionary to China which had just opened for missionary work. He received a letter stating, "I have learned that our bishops are at a loss for at least two suitable young men to go to China. My mind has turned to yourself as better qualified for such an undertaking than any others that I know." On June 20, 1847 Robert wrote, "You are at liberty to present my name to the bishop for appointment in China." As his family waved fond farewells, Robert rode out over the hills of Concord, wondering if he would ever see his loved ones or homeland again. His destiny lay halfway around the world.

After a long and difficult journey, Robert arrived in Foochow, where no one he met knew a word of English and where there was a natural suspicion of foreigners. Lonely, Robert longed for a woman to share his life. There are several stories regarding his courtship of Henrietta Caroline Sperry. In one, it was said that he wrote to the Board of Missions for help in obtaining a wife.

A young woman whom the board felt would be suitable was selected and correspondence between the two began. Photographs were exchanged, and the brave young woman boarded a ship for China. In the other version, the woman who became his wife was already a well-loved friend. Whatever version is correct, Henrietta proved to be an exceptional helpmate. The strength of her faith is revealed in a comment overheard in later years when she placed her children on board the ship to come to the States for their education, "Dear Jesus, I do this all for Thee."

Rev. and Mrs. Maclay ministered in China and in 1856 two Methodist churches were erected there. Robert created a Chinese alphabetic dictionary and wrote a book on life in China. In 1871, after twenty-seven years of service, Maclay was appointed superintendent of a new mission in Japan. He translated a large portion of the New Testament into Japanese and then was asked to prepare the way for a mission in Korea. Retiring from the mission field in 1887, he returned to San Fernanado to become dean of the Maclay School of Theology. The faith and Christian fervor of the Maclay family was exceptional.

David Ferguson, an elder in the United Presbyterian Church, had two grandchildren who entered the ministry and one granddaughter who became a missionary. Thomas Ferguson served the Silver Spring Presbyterian Church outside Harrisburg for fifty years and served several terms in the state legislature. His brother, Gracey Ferguson, became president of Westminster College in New Wilmington after serving churches in Mercersburg and Butler. Tom and Gracey's only sister, Ann, married Rev. George McCormick, and they became missionaries in California after the Civil War, planting a number of churches. Other descendants of David Ferguson have also been ministers in the Presbyterian Church; Huber and Jim Ferguson in Pittsburgh; Harry Ferguson, Jr. in Waterloo; and David Dunn who served as dean of the Lancaster Theological Seminary. A fifth-generation descendant, Alice Hope, broke into the ranks as the 12th woman to graduate from Princeton Seminary with a Master of Divinity degree and served churches in New Jersey and Pennsylvania.

The staunch faith and commitment of these early Presbyterians and Methodists was evident in many ways. When the Noss family home caught fire, only one piece of furniture was saved. Mr. Noss gave the chair to the Methodist Church at Waterloo, saying it was all he had left, and he would give it to the Lord. Many practiced tithing, giving a tenth of their income to the church.

There was often an unexpected humorous element in church services, whether Presbyterian or Methodist. Cats must have been plentiful in Concord because they attended services of both denominations. Ms. McKim related an incident that caused quite a stir in the Methodist Church. A cat got his head caught in the pitcher used to replenish the minister's drinking glass. With great effort, the cat managed to distract the worshipers by extricating himself from the pitcher in a frantic act that sent glass flying in all directions.

During one Presbyterian service when the prayer was long and ardent, the cat drank the communion wine to the consternation of the minister. The cat, after considerable purring, made a tipsy exit.

EDUCATION

A passionate religious faith characterized the lives of many Scots-Irish and was equaled by a zeal for education. Many of the early pioneers in Concord were avid readers. In addition to the Bible, some, like the Linn family, were fortunate enough to own Bunyan's *Pilgrim's Progress*, *Aesop's Fables*, Plutarch's *Lives*, the *Essays of Bacon and Addison*, Milton's *Paradise Lost*, Rollin's *Ancient History*, Fox's *Book of Martyrs*, and perhaps Shakespeare or Locke's "*Essay Concerning Human Understanding.*" Such books were read and re-read forming the backdrop of how he or she looked at the world.

In order to obtain a good education for their children, parents in Concord banded together to hire a teacher. In a small log cabin without plaster or proper ceiling with two holes covered with oiled paper that served as windows, children learned to read, write, and cipher.

Teachers leave an indelible imprint on the lives of their students, and memories live on. Mr. William Smiley who taught in the valley in the 1830s was described as a man of "highest principles of honesty and integrity discharging every duty with a conscientious regard for his temporal and eternal well being." Despite his frequent application of the rod, he was kind and tender-hearted. When a six-year-old student fell into a pot of boiling water and suffered severe burns, Smiley carried the lad to and from school for a number of weeks so that he could continue his studies and see his classmates. Mr. Charles Widney and Mr. Lyons followed Mr. Smiley.

Concord had a school for approximately forty years before the passage of the Free or Public School System Act in 1835. Located on the mountain road to Perry County, the school was so close to the road and "heavy traffic," that the teacher had to check the road before releasing the children. At times, one teacher was responsible for seventy to eighty students.

The school was built of logs, the roof covered with boards. The interior was described as cheerless and dreary. Light and ventilation came from windows which were single panes of glass inserted at intervals around three sides of the building. Writing desks were arranged below these windows and occupied by older and larger scholars. Younger students sat on benches in the center of the room where they were more closely supervised and closer to the source of heat in winter.

In warm weather, flies also attended, buzzing noisily. Students brought their lunches and to quench their thirst drank from McKim's watering trough shared by man and beast alike. Furthermore, this was not a day of indoor plumbing. As one teacher pointed out, "Sanitary conditions were not up to present day conditions."

Later, as needs increased a two-story frame structure was built and heated by two ten-plate stoves. Unfortunately, the building caught fire and burned down. Almost everyone in town, wakened by the dancing flames, gathered around the site. Oscar Little, in his brief history of Concord wrote, "With tear filled eyes we watched its timbers crumble, but we still cherish its pleasant memories." The zeal for education brought the community together and another school building was quickly raised.

In many ways, the school functioned as a community center. There were spelling bees, singing schools, and entertainments of various kinds. Although life was hard, it was not without its pleasures.

In 1863, the Waterloo Academy opened its doors, providing another educational opportunity. Its advertisement read, "The object of the proprietor is to afford a cheap and quiet high school near home where parents may have oversight of their children and have them apart from those exciting scenes which distract the minds of pupils in all large institutions." Two sessions were offered. Room and board per week cost $1.75. Courses offered were as follows: Common English, $6.00; Higher English, $8.00; Drawing, Painting, Watercolors, $5.00; Painting in Oil Colors, $10.00: Music on Piano, $10.00; Use of Piano, $4.00; Miss Anna Graham was principal and Mrs. Sara Campbell was her assistant. William Campbell was the proprietor.

POLITICS

Faith, education, and love of freedom resulted in a dynamic discussion of politics. The Scots-Irish were described as "firm in belief, theologically erudite, and aware of the trend of the times." Debates were long and loud and took place when people met on the road, at the post office, and in the stores. No matter the party affiliation, constituents' opinions differed on how things were being handled by Congress.

As an example, Squire Harris, William McKinzie, and David Ferguson were among the early settlers and were great friends, but they differed politically, religiously, and in personality. Harris was a Republican, Ferguson and McKinzie, Democrats. Harris and Ferguson were Presbyterians, McKinzie a Roman Catholic. McKinzie was known for his "considerable horse sense and Irish wit." Harris was characterized as a man who was not happy with a man "who knew nothing." Yet these three were often seen together both arguing and laughing.

As a further illustration, Robert Maclay, a devoted Methodist, described John Doyle as a devout Catholic and an "excellent man," stating that he "enjoyed religious conversation with him and felt sure that they would see exactly alike in Heaven." Differences of opinion did not destroy community life.

There were debating societies to sharpen the mind. In log books from the 1800s, one finds not only the price of store items and the names of those who purchased them, but also scribbled notes for a future debate.

> Ladies and Gentlemen…The subject for this evening's discussion is one that should interest us all, one in which we should feel more or less interest. Resolved that peace is mightier than the sword. As I am on the negative side, I shall endeavor to show that more deeds of heroism have been accomplished and more done to civilize the country through the use of weapons of warfare…First, as a civilization we have only to refer you to the War of Revolution in which the feeble colonists threw off the British yoke of bondage and by the use of the sword laid the foundation for one of the greatest and grandest countries the sun ever shone upon, on the country we all feel proud of, and I delight in claiming the home of the free and the brave.

Keeping store and preparing for a debate apparently were all part of life in the community.

A number of descendants of the original inhabitants of this small town played a role in politics. David Ferguson's son, James, became an associate judge in Franklin County and his grandson, Tom, served in the Pennsylvania legislature. Charles Maclay, son of Robert, moved to California about 1851 and served two terms in the state senate. James Campbell's son, Alexander, moved to Illinois and served as a member of Congress in 1850 and 1858. Edward Doyle served as a county commissioner.

Community activities in Concord included the short life span of Freemasonry. Started by stonemasons in York, England in 1717, lodges later appeared in Ireland and Scotland. Many of the early settlers had probably been Masons in their native land. Benjamin Franklin and George Washington were prominent members. Lodges began with a group of men of similar interests who met annually to carry on business, usually devoted to charitable ends.

On August 9, 1797, John Johnson, Thomas Wright and James Widney petitioned the Grand Lodge in Philadelphia for permission to organize a lodge in Concord. By 1798, thirteen members transferred from other lodges. Nine were new recruits, James Campbell among them. The group met in the upper floor of the large brick house opposite the post office. Of the twenty-five, ten withdrew during 1799 and by 1800 Lodge Number 74 had breathed its last.

BUSINESSES

Businesses began to flourish. The mill was first and drew others to Concord. Records are sketchy, but we know there was a mill owned by James McMullin, inherited from his grandfather Eneas, located on land south of the creek.

In 1810, Linns built a mill on the west end of the bridge. The structure was a log building "38 feet by 40 feet, two and one-half stories high with a 12 foot overshot water wheel, and two stands of buhrs and bolts for wheat and buckwheat flour." A sturdy building, the floors were of pine boards one and a quarter inches in thickness and many of them more than twenty inches wide. Shaved white pine shingles covered the roof. The water wheel made of oak was impressive in size; four feet six inches wide and twelve feet high. In the east corner of the ground floor was a room known as the mill room. Oscar Little described the room. "A bunk covered with deer skin, a small desk where the books were kept and two chairs that had been in use so long the legs were worn off up to the rungs, constituted the mill room."

In those days, the custom was to take grain to the mill and leave it for several days while the miller ground it into flour taking one-tenth of the grain for his pay. If a farmer brought in grain that was not clean, it was returned to him.

James Widney Linn bought his father's mill and made his reputation as a superior workman. Strictly keeping the Sabbath, Linn often ran the mill from 1 a.m. Monday morning until 11 p.m. Saturday night.

In 1866, James Little purchased the mill from the Linn's, along with ten acres of land. Among the millers he employed were John Harris, John Conn, John Weight, and S. Little. Oscar Little purchased the mill in 1912. It shut down in 1916.

Along the Tuscarora Creek from the Narrows to a point near the source of the stream, the following mills were once in operation: Little's at Concord, Weldy's near James Robertson's farm house, Coulter's on Chill Robertson's farm, and Rhone's on the crossroad beyond Doylesburg. The latter became known as McLaughlin's Mill. There was also mention of a flax mill on the creek below the Gamble home.

The lovely stone bridge south of Concord on the Back Road running parallel to the Tuscarora Mountain and Route 75 was built in 1832 by John Weaver at a cost of $1,800. It held up well and was repaired in August 1911 by Frank Harry. Its lovely arches span the Tuscarora Creek.

Concord was a bustling place. The Erwin, Maclay, and Harris families had tanneries which at times produced unsavory odors. The Harris tannery was at the north end of town near the Narrows. Parents continually warned their inquisitive offspring to stay away from the waste pits.

A foundry and plow shop were owned by the McKim's. One can imagine the din this business produced, echoing back and forth through the hills. The men who worked at the foundry were required to wear (the somewhat fire retardant) woolen clothes and stockings. Iron "frogs" used as doorstops, bells, boot-pullers in the shape of a little black boy lying down, and bullets, were among the products the foundry produced. When times were desperate, some brought their old pewter spoons to melt which were used in the process of making bullets. A big cannon ball was manufactured when Franklin County was overrun by Confederate forces during the Civil War.

One of the oldest landmarks was the James Harris' shoemaker shop. Constructed of logs and roofed with shaved oak shingles, the shop had benches for two shoemakers. Around the walls were racks for large rolls of sole leather which customers brought to the shop and left to be used for their family's footwear as the need arose. In the corner were a hand operated cider press and several barrels containing vinegar. The loft of the shop served as a smokehouse where the villagers brought their meat to be processed. The owner of the meat put his initials on the back or skin side of the meat with paint, or if paint was not available, a colored string was woven through the small end of the cut. The contents of the loft were worth more in January through March than the building itself. Although fathers were opposed to their boys loafing in the village store, they did not object to them going to the shoemaker's shop. As one boy reported, "We spent many happy hours there, sampling the fresh cider and listening to stories of old times as told by the aged shoemaker."

John Johnston built the first general store in the village selling a variety of dry goods, followed by John Little who bought the property. The Seibert family opened a wagon shop and the Noble family a coach shop. Alexander Erwin operated a sawmill. The cabinet shop was owned by the Orrs. Philip McElheney's harness shop was always busy. There were three shoemakers, and a cigar manufacturer. James Wilson was both a chair maker and undertaker, serving in those capacities for more than forty years. John Little continued the business. Both Little and Donnelly families ran smith shops.

The blacksmith was an institution in every village. Odds and ends of iron, old wheels, and discarded horseshoes littered the floor. In the midst of the clutter stood the blacksmith, working with one hand on the bellows and the other holding the iron implement in the fire, intent on his business. Eric Sloane writes, "He was the sage of the community, the boy's best friend, and a philosopher as well. He fixed bicycles, repaired wagons, sharpened skates and earned the love of all small boys who were his audience."

Every town probably had what some would call a "town character." In the case of Concord, it was the eccentric photographer who named himself John Penn. He apparently believed that he owned Pennsylvania. Sporting a long, flowing beard usually parted in the middle, he rarely appeared on the street unless clad in a frock coat, oxfords, spats and a high silk hat.

In reality, John Penn was John Wesley Calvin Goshorn born near Nossville, Huntingdon County. According to the story, his mother not only named him after the founders of the Methodist (Wesley) and Presbyterian (Calvin) churches but was determined he would become a minister of the gospel.

Goshorn entered Bucknell University where his overreaching ambition to be at the top of his class resulted in a nervous breakdown from which he never entirely recovered.

Upon the death of his father, Goshorn and his mother moved to Concord. Apparently, being something of an artist he painted a portrait of his father and preached the funeral sermon with the portrait placed in front of the pulpit. Later, he purchased a double stone house and a small frame house where he operated a drugstore filled with cures to which teetotalers objected. Many customers had colds that nothing but rock candy and whiskey could cure. A few citizens took umbrage, and Judge Stewart put an end to the enterprise.

John Penn's somewhat odd creativity was endless. He converted an old building into an opera house with a sign reading, "Sacred Opera" in large letters on the front of the building. Later it was named "Chancel Hall" and finally "Chantilly Place." No revenue resulted. Perhaps the green snake with a protruding tongue painted on the wall kept people away.

Following the example of his brother, a newspaper editor in Washington, D.C., Penn then went into the printing business. He also worked for a short time as editor of the *Concord News*. If the public expressed any displeasure with the content of his articles, he spent the night printing a rebuttal, targeting specific townspeople. His neighbors felt vulnerable, intrigued, and sometimes frightened by him. His brother finally had him committed to a mental institution where he remained for a short time. After his release, he was hired by an engraving company. According to some historians, John Goshorn is buried in Concord.

Fortunately, the town did not have to depend on John Penn's drugstore during these years. Dr. John Davis was a Concord physician prior to 1825. When he moved west, Dr. Crawford, who lived in the stone house on the diamond, served the community between 1820 and 1848, traveling day and night over rough roads to treat the sick, deliver babies, and bring comfort to the ailing. Eventually, there was a dentist by the name of Irvine Andrews who served the area.

There were hotels where people gathered to drink away their woes. As one disgruntled townsman said, "In days gone by the town was cursed by two licensed hotels." Brawls broke out, and arguments were settled by force. Men lined up on both sides of the road around the diamond to watch the altercations which usually took place on Saturday nights. It was said that "the fellow that could get home without help was usually declared the winner." Ladies stayed inside after dark, but many watched from behind curtained windows.

A resident of Burns Valley once traded a chicken for liquor at the Concord Hotel. The landlord sent him to the coop with the chicken. Unobserved, every time the man got thirsty he went to the coop and retrieved the chicken trading it for more liquor. He drank all evening on one fowl. When the landlord went to his coop the next morning, he expected to find many nice chickens but found only one! On another night, one man was so drunk he attempted to hitch his wagon to the tail of his horse. In his befuddled state, he wasn't sure which was the front end or the back!

Drinking was common and played a role in hospitality in those early days. There were a few, however, who could not control their thirst and in another era would be considered alcoholics. A story was told about a drunk walking down the street one night and happened to look through a window. He overheard Mr. Pomeroy say, "Mr. Linn, it is a very chilly evening. Won't you take something to drink before going?" Mr. Linn accepted. As he was leaving, he was accosted by the drunk who greeted him like a brother. Well, Mr. Linn, I see you are fond of a little whiskey, too." The comment cut Mr. Linn to the quick. To think that even inadvertently, his action might encourage a man to drink! He vowed total abstinence and never took another drink.

A widow, Mrs. William McElhenny, was described as someone who "knew how to keep a hotel." There were no complaints of disorder or violation of license laws at her establishment which someone noted "was more than could be said for her male competitors." Apparently, Mrs. McElhenny was preceded by the first hotel keeper, James Widney, Jr. Among others in the hotel business were Edward Doyle and H. Miller who was proprietor of the "Valley Home Hotel."

The problem of communication between valley towns and the outside world was finally addressed with the arrival of the postal service which created great excitement. In 1789, George Washington appointed the first

Postmaster General, but it was not until January 16, 1811 that a post office was established in Concord. Mail was carried once every two weeks between Fannettsburg and Mifflintown. Postage was six cents for every thirty miles. Edward W. Doyle was the first postmaster, succeeded by James Wilson.

The area lacked newspapers until the Civil War years. The *Concord Pioneer* was published by G. B. Goshorn and David Goshorn. The name was changed after May 1863 to *The Union*. The date on one preserved paper reads June 1862. Inside is the statement, "The Pioneer is a strictly independent Monthly Journal, devoted to General and Local Intelligence, Education, Poetry, Tales, Anecdotes, Advertising and so forth and pledged to the support of the interests of the community in which it circulates irrespective of Party prejudice or Sectarianism." The subscription rate was twenty-five cents a year.

The newspaper kept the public informed about the events of the Civil War which occupied two center pages. Among other content were death notices and market prices. We learn that in 1862, eggs sold for eight cents a dozen and butter was ten cents a pound. There was a notice that "S. B. Hockenberry had returned from the City with a large stock of Goods, Cheaper than the cheapest Goods for the Ladies." The schedules of the stagecoach and various town activities were also listed. This issue announced that the Literary Association was "in very prosperous condition and good will seemed to pervade all present." Members listed were David Goshorn, George W. Linn, William H. Bratton, R. M. Donnelly, J. W. Goshorn, R. A. Campbell, J. M. Donnelly, S. H. Wilson, Thomas A. Doyle, J. W. Campbell, J. A. Johnson, John H. Little, J. B. Erwin, J. W. Robertson, and H. W. Linn.

In the meantime, roads needed improvement. The narrow trail through the Narrows had been in use as a road but was located high on one side of the mountain. Making a sharp bend through a covered bridge spanning the creek, it bent back sharply on the other side. Some called the high portion, Cape Horn Road which was connected to another trail that came out near the Love farm and was used when the creek was high and the area flooded.

By 1830, the state had appropriated money to build a road from Path Valley over the Kittochtinny Mountain into Sherman's Valley, Perry County.

Times were hard and money was scarce. Eager for work, men lined up. They were paid fifty cents per day, furnished their own shovels and picks, and looked after their own room and board. The road was greatly improved, but for the most part remained an improved bridle path.

Sometimes there was great excitement in the community. A man by the name of Jack Drumm believed he had discovered gold in the Narrows. Working through two tons of rock, he extricated $2.00 worth of gold. With that amount of labor required, no one was willing to invest in further exploration. There were also rumors of a silver deposit in back of Waterloo. People kept hoping, but it never materialized. One day, a man came into town filled with excitement and announced, "We've discovered an oil well! As it turned out, someone had intentionally placed an oil-soaked cloth near a spring which tainted the water and gave it an oily sheen. At another time, a seam of coal was found, and this caused considerable excitement. Explorers discovered, to their disappointment, it was only twenty-two inches thick and eighty to a hundred feet long. There was, however, plenty of stone.

Meanwhile, about eleven stone houses were built. Unlike other areas in Franklin County, stone was plentiful in the Concord Narrows. Scots were known for their ability as stone masons, and it was said that a Scot could not stop building until there was not one stone left. Later, clay was discovered along the creek providing excellent material for making brick as one can see from the two churches in town.

The McKim house revealed three progressive periods of building history; the first log on the north side, then stone and finally frame. The Robert Maclay house, built in 1790, was described as a structure of large hand hewn cedar logs chinked with stones and mortar, the distinctive aroma of cedar pervading the house from basement to attic. There was a huge fireplace in the basement which could accommodate several cranes used to support cooking pots over the fire. Later, the Pomeroys owned the property and the space housed a dry goods store and the town's first post office. The Alexander Erwin house, built in 1797, was known as a house of "unusual elegance." Located on a hill at the north edge of town, it featured a massive twelve-foot square central chimney.

The house had no fewer than six fireplaces including one on the third floor. Mary Shearer of East Waterford remembered the Erwin family talk about runaway slaves hidden by the occupants in a windowless basement room. Norman Gamble, who grew up in the house, described the back door being secured by two heavy wooden bars pushed through iron brackets mounted on the wall as a protection against Indians. At one time, there was a plate giving the date of the home's construction, but it disappeared. Unfortunately, the old and lovely structure fell victim to arson in April 1980. The 500 acre estate remained in the Erwin family for more than a century.

COMMUNITY

Just as Concord was once known for its lovely old homes, Concord women were known for their decorum. As life in Concord settled into a rhythm, well established women finished their work in the morning, and dressed in their best and were ready for afternoon tea. On formal outings, women wore hats and white gloves. They had overcome their more humble beginnings. Now they could afford fashion magazines and read of life in less rural areas.

From existing records come unusual stories of romances gone awry. For some reason, the Erwin family would not allow their daughter Mary to marry John Lauthers. She was sent away to live with an aunt, a doctor in Mexico. Homesick and lovesick, she pined away. Finally, her father relented, sent for John, and told him Mary was coming home. It was not to end happily, however. John was by then engaged to another woman. Heartbroken, Mary returned and after a period of time married Herbert Gamble and happily raised a number of children.

The Nailer family was a good illustration of family feuds and its effects on the love lives of the young of that day. A young lass fell in love with a lad, but the Nailor's refused to let her marry, in spite of the fact that the wedding dress was prepared and the ring was on her finger. The bride-to-be was overwhelmed, eventually fell into a coma, and presumed dead. She was buried in her wedding dress in the cemetery near the Presbyterian Church. Her fiancée, who had been unable to visit her during her illness was overwhelmed with grief, dug up the coffin that night so that he could see her once more. As he tried to take the ring from her swollen finger, she moaned. Frightened, he fled to the road where he fell on the ground and passed out.

As it happened, the bride's grandfather was on the road to Richmond Furnace. He stopped his wagon, examined the young man, and revived him with whiskey. Incoherently and babbling, the heartbroken boy pointed to the graveyard. The girl was discovered sitting on the steps of the church, her bleeding finger wrapped in her wedding veil.

The grandfather took pity on the young couple and hid them in the straw on the wagon. At Richmond Furnace, he bought his granddaughter a plain dress, put the couple on the train and handed them $80, telling them to go as far as they could. According to the story, the grandfather quickly returned to the cemetery, closed the coffin and filled in the hole. A stone monument was later erected at the grave.

Years later, a woman and three boys came in by train and stopped at East Waterford. On their way to Concord, they visited the grave. At a church service, one of the boys revealed that he had been born twenty-one years *after his mother had been buried*. Following the service, they quickly left the area. The story appeared as a fragment in a Presbyterian Church history.

James Widney's dream of a town had come true. The town was bustling with activity and rapidly becoming a thriving commercial center. Old log books reveal that people came over the mountain from Perry County and through the Narrows from Juniata and Huntingdon counties to purchase items, use the various services, enjoy community activities and visit. Concord was a lively place in the first half of the 1800's, and the story was only beginning.

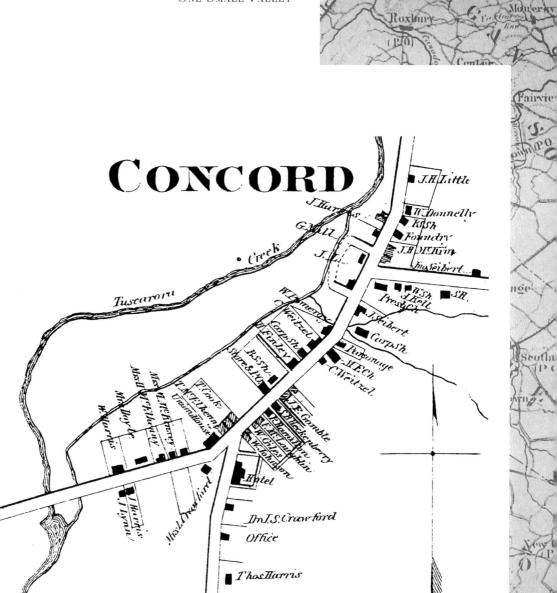

Map of Concord from D. G. Beers'
Atlas of Franklin County, 1868.

Tannery and covered bridge north
of Concord from the mouth
of Horse Valley.

The Methodist Episcopal Church
was built in the 1850s..

The United Presbyterian Church
was built in 1850.

The Erwin House stood
on the hill north of
Concord. It was known for
its beautiful architecture
but fell victim to arson.

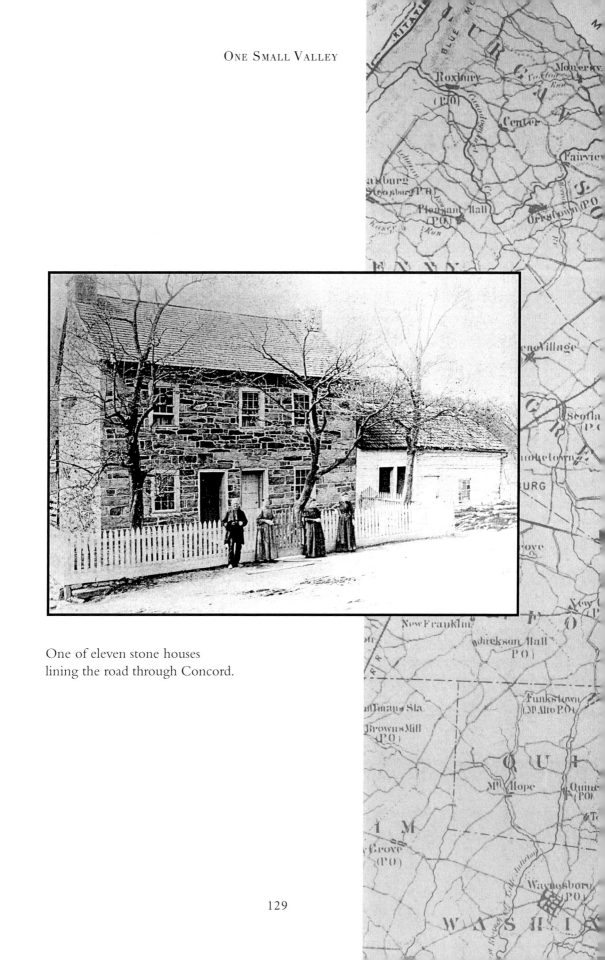

One of eleven stone houses
lining the road through Concord.

This early Widney House stood on the
hill south of Concord.

The McKim House, with its
original log end, is still standing.

130

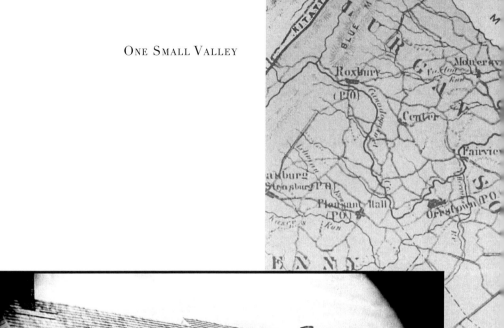

An early inn on the west side
of the Concord diamond
during festivities.

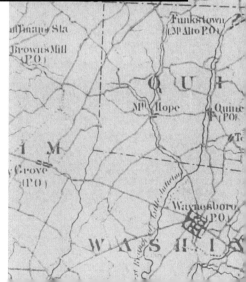

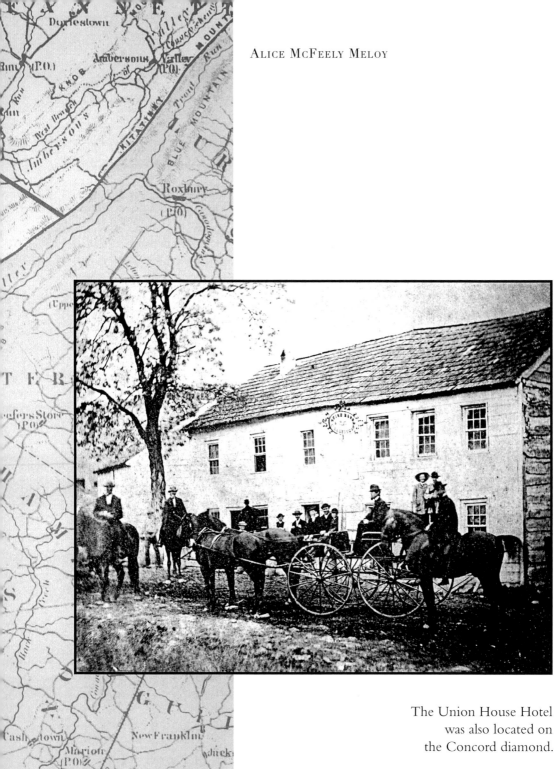

The Union House Hotel
was also located on
the Concord diamond.

DOYLESBURG

CHAPTER TEN

DOYLESTOWN WAS IN EXISTENCE long before Doylesburg was founded in 1851. Both were named after the Doyle family, who had acquired a large tract of land in the center of the valley north of Dry Run. Mary McNesby, former owner of the large stone house in Doylestown, had in her possession a land warrant dated 1758 for 580 acres. The spring found in this area had once been the site of a fort as mentioned elsewhere.

One of the original log houses was attached to the McNesby home until it was removed in 1938, but a log springhouse still stands. A second stone house standing on the hill is of early vintage and belongs to Gerald Best, a descendant of the Doyle family. A third house has been built around the original log cabin which includes a large walk-in fireplace.

The Doyle family has a long and interesting history. After buying their land from the Indians, they settled around 1734, were evicted, returned in time for the French and Indian War and built a fort. Barnabas and Patrick Doyle fought in the Revolution. Patrick also fought in the War of 1812. Many people whose ancestors lived in Path Valley carry their genes.

The Doyles were faithful Roman Catholics and played an important role in bringing Roman Catholicism to the valley. Mass was first celebrated in 1790 at the Timmons homestead, located on the corner of Route 641 and the Mill Road on the west branch of the Conococheague Creek. The Shield, Rease, Fegan, Price, and Hagie families also opened their homes for worship and communion when a priest was available.

In the year 1802, the Roman Catholics of the area built a log church on land that belonged to Barnabas Doyle. After his death, the land was deeded to the Catholic Church by his widow, Mary McElheney Doyle and their children. The "deed of gift" included land to enlarge the cemetery.

Families from Amberson now crossed the mountain to attend Mass in the log church. Walking the rocky trail in bare feet to preserve their Sunday shoes, these early settlers waited to put their shoes on until they were within sight of the church.

In 1820, Father Kerns became the first resident pastor of Corpus Christi Catholic Church in Chambersburg and served once a month in Path Valley until 1849. By 1842, there were about twenty-three families on the church roll. At that time, Father Martin Kelly took residence and spent the entire year in Path Valley.

Between 1840 and 1850, members decided to replace the log church with a brick structure. Members prepared the rocks, laid the foundation, molded and baked the bricks, finding suitable material on the Fegan home-stead. They felled and hauled wood for the beams and applied the plaster. According to oral history, the names of some of those early members and builders were written on a hidden roof beam. Members were so generous in their giving that the church was paid for before the work began. As one person wrote, "The history of the parish was a record of its lay members rather than its clerical leaders."

The church was blessed by Father Myers of Hagerstown on November 13, 1853 and dedicated to Saint Mary, Refuge of Sinners. During a visit in

1854, Father Louis J. Miller blessed the cemetery while Bishop Neumann heard confessions in "German, Irish, and English." Marriages were celebrated, the sick were visited, and in 1857 forty-one communicants were confirmed during a bishop's visit. By 1863, there were forty-nine members in Amberson Valley and one hundred and forty-nine in Path Valley. The church was growing and so was the Doyle family who continued to make contributions to the valley and areas beyond.

The Coulters were also early settlers. There is an unconfirmed mention of a Coulter fort at the base of the Round Top and the name of Lieutenant Richard Coulter appears on signed petitions both in May and June of 1778 and in February 1779. One petition was for rifles. Muskets were not effective in the woods when fighting Indians. In the second, we find a request for guards to either "reap the grain, guard the forts or scout the woods behind us."

In all likelihood, this is the same Richard Coulter who transacted a land warrant from John Coulter of Cumberland County, dated November 29, 1786. The tract was large and located in the area that would later become Doylesburg.

A Samuel Coulter served as private under Captain Thomas Askey. His will is dated 1793. In it he named a wife, Margaret, and among his listed children were sons Samuel and Matthew who became founders of a prosperous business located at the foot of the Round Top. In the first half of the 1800's, the Coulter enterprise grew rapidly. There was a tannery, a still, a mill, the farm and numerous other businesses. With the grain they bought in Juniata County, their wagons were constantly en route to Baltimore. Selling the grain, they brought store goods and necessities such as salt, sugar, and iron for the return trip. Carrying money on these trips meant hiring an armed guard to ride with them. They carried their cash by pack horse to the Chambersburg bank which opened in 1809.

Strangely enough, while they made money (and also operated a lucrative still), there was a Rev. Richard Coulter in Juniata, licensed by New Castle Presbytery in 1798, who came to Middle Tuscarora Church as a missionary. When he arrived, it was "about as common to use intoxicating beverages as it was to drink water." There was rum at funerals lest one seem inhospitable. Rum was served when the minister was installed. A minister could be slightly inebriated and found acceptable, but if found whistling on Sunday could be defrocked. Rev. Coulter believed that it was "a sin and a shame to pollute the atmosphere of God's house with the fumes of a bar-room." He set forth to remedy the situation, insisting that the church should be a great temperance society. He organized the first of these in the valley at the Lower Tuscarora Presbyterian Church in 1831.

Rev. Coulter was the first to banish rum from the harvest field where it had been regarded as indispensable for reviving weary reapers. When it came time to harvest his own crop, only one man would consent to work for him without alcohol, but Rev. Coulter was adamant. The crop could rot then. He offered good buttermilk instead. In spite of his stand against alcohol, 357 members were added to his church during his long ministry. Such are the ironies of the Coulter family history. Matthew, Samuel, and Margaret were members of the Upper Path Valley Presbyterian Church.

The Coulter holdings extended south of what would become Doylesburg. In recent years, the land located a short distance north of Doylestown was known as the Ryder farm. James Goshorn owned it for a number of years. The original log house was located behind the sturdy red brick house which has a spring in the basement.

Meanwhile, during these years, the Coulters continued to expand their business empire while drawing up plans for their retirement home. The ground on which they planned to build belonged to Peter Foreman, a Revolutionary War veteran, and his wife Esther. The deed for the property is dated 1792. In 1810, Foreman sold sixteen acres to Matthew and Samuel Coulter for $350 and bought a farm in Burns Valley. The land the Coulter's bought was adjacent to holdings belonging to William Taylor and Joseph Moore.

Building a retirement house proved no small job. With the Coulters' exposure to southern architecture on their business trips to Baltimore, the retirement home was to have double porches, fancy trim and elegant moldings inside. Incorporated into the framework were some of the sturdy pegged beams of Peter Foreman's cabin. Molding was imported and brought by pack horses. Plasterers capable of creating ornamentation on the ceilings and other workmen with special skills were also brought in. According to reports, finished lumber was brought from Carlisle and building went on apace. Originally, the shutters were painted green and the porches, red. The Coulters not only imported furniture from Britain, but according to legend held fox hunts riding over the fields in the style of landed gentry. From all reports, the Coulters enjoyed their retirement and wealth. They sold the farming enterprise to William and Childerson Robertson in 1851.

During the Confederate occupation of Franklin County before the Battle of Gettysburg, some marauding soldiers not only found their way into Path Valley but ventured as far as Burns Valley, rounding up horses and cattle. A neighbor stopped by the Coulter home to share the news and found Matthew in the cellar, frantically burying his gold.

The era of the Coulters came to an end with the deaths of Samuel in 1856 and Matthew in 1863, at the age of ninety. Other members of the family had moved to Illinois. The retirement house was sold on December 18, 1867 to Harmon (or Herman) Hockenberry for $1,300. Some say it was converted to a tavern; others say it became a Conestoga wagon stop.

Another early settler, Catherine Campbell Hamilton Robertson from Glasgow, a descendant of Sir Colin Campbell of Ardkinlass, married William Hamilton, and with their two young boys came to Philadelphia, where Hamilton worked in the mercantile business. Unfortunately, yellow fever, a dreaded and often fatal disease, killed her young husband. A woman of courage, Catherine escaped the city which was under quarantine and started out for Path Valley where she had a relative or a friend from home. According to the story, she and her two boys walked most of the way. In time, William Robertson who had met her at a friend's house in either Scotland or Philadelphia, followed her to Path Valley. They married and started farming in Burns Valley where he hung out his shingle as a tailor. They had a large family. It was three of their children, William, Childerson and Katherine who settled on the farm purchased from the Coulter family.

The Coulter retirement home was on the market again and in 1879 was bought by Squire Robertson. Descendants of William and Catherine Robertson were buying land around the Round Top and during the next century, there would be Robertson farms from Squire Robertson's house to Concord. The area became a little Scotland, the dream of their Argyle ancestors.

A branch of the Campbell clan settled in the same area. Like so many other early settlers, they too came from County Fermanagh in Ireland, having emigrated there from Scotland.

James Campbell, a weaver, married Martha Robinson and brought his family to America in 1796. Their fourth child, John, was born at sea. Landing in Philadelphia, they bought land in Perry County. Acquainted with the Johnston, Widney, and Linn families when they were neighbors in Ireland, they renewed their friendship. In 1824, John Campbell married Ann Johnston. They settled in Burns Valley in 1831.

The Campbell clan was known for its wealth. In time, Hance Campbell, part of the Perry County clan of Campbells and Johnsons, all good Presbyterians, became owner of a large tract of land in Burns Valley. Called Big Hance, he was nicknamed "King of Burns Valley." His farming operation was large and required the labor of many hands.

The men who married while working for Hance received as a wedding gift, a cow, a plot of land, and help with building a cabin. Many by the name of Hockenberry lived in Burns Valley and worked for Hance. According to some, the Hockenberry family was of French extraction and known as a handsome group of people.

Hance's brother, Robert, was not as wealthy as Hance and did not live in Burns Valley, but reared two boys and two girls in a cabin with a dirt floor. Every spring and fall, Hance visited Robert, bringing with him a big bag of flour and a ham. Robert's boys became well-known as Dr. William Campbell and Dr. Robert Campbell. Both lived in Huntingdon County. This branch of the family remained Presbyterian while Hance's descendents eventually became Methodists.

The red brick house north of the present town of Doylesburg on Route 75 has long been associated with the Campbell name, and has a long and fascinating story. The small stone house behind the main house was probably part of the original dwelling. On the beam above the fireplace is scratched the date 176? The faint number appears to be a five. A log structure was connected to the stone house at one time and was probably the first dwelling. Exactly when the property became home to the Taylor's is unknown.

According to the Taylor family history, it was from this site that little Susan Taylor was carried away by the Indians. Her mother looked out in time to see little Susan, her red hair shining in the sun, looking back over the shoulder of an Indian. Neighbors quickly gathered and set out in pursuit, but the little girl was never found. Every generation of Taylors since then has named one child Susan in her memory.

In 1801, Thomas Taylor built the big brick house. There are indications that the house served as a tavern sometime before 1830. The dimension of the rooms and the sliding doors on the second floor lend credence to stories of parties, dances, and romances. According to oral history, young ladies with wide skirts rode side-saddle from Path Valley, Perry County and other areas to attend dances there. Descendants in the area have recalled how gracefully they slipped from the horses, landing lightly on the stepping stones, their full skirts flowing. As the fiddles played and the dancing began, romances flourished.

Squire Taylor was injured in an accident at the brick kiln and sent away for schooling. He later became a justice of the peace. Many weddings took place in the house. Wills were probated and deeds transferred. It was a busy place!

The road in front of the house was often filled with the rumble of wagons belonging to the Leonard's of Juniata or the Coulter's, both on their way to Baltimore. Horses churned up the dust and the chatter and songs of travelers filled the air. By mid-century, a stagecoach would go rattling by, en route from Concord to Fannettsburg.

For a short period of time at mid-century, Methodists held worship services in the Taylor house, where Wesley's hymns were enthusiastically sung and dreams of a Methodist church in Doylesburg grew. During the second half of the 1800's, the McVitty family added an addition on the southern side of the brick house. The Taylor/McVitty house later became home for the Fred Campbell clan for several lively generations, as the Campbells spread over the valley and took leadership roles.

The town of Doylesburg was laid out in 1851 by Philip Doyle, who operated the first post office and store. Mail came from Amberson and Roxbury twice a week. A tannery with a capacity of 6,000 hides south of town was owned by William and James McLean and bustled with activity. K. Rosenberry served as superintendent of the operation. Soon there was a blacksmith on the southern edge of town and a shoe shop on the north end. In 1864, Dr. Isaac Clugston, known as an herb doctor, started a store that would become a big operation under the supervision of his son, Alva.

With prosperity came the need for education. Public schools were established. The Burns Valley School was located under a big oak tree near a spring a mile or so from the intersection of Route 75 and Route 274. Here many children in the area learned to read, write, and cipher. At Christmas, students climbed the slopes near the school to collect pine and bittersweet to decorate the school house. There were poems to be memorized and parents to invite to hear recitations. Eventually, a second school was located on the edge of Doylesburg along the crossroad. In time, Ryder's School opened farther down the road. These schools offered classes from first through eighth grade.

In this mountainous area, exciting and unexpected things happened. A newspaper reported that young Alice Peck, daughter of George Peck, had wandered away from home and disappeared into the mountains that divide Franklin and Perry counties. Apparently, she had followed an old bark road to its end. From there all traces of her disappeared. Day and night, the anxious father with the aid of his neighbors and then as many as two hundred more men, searched the area, to no avail. Hours passed as the searchers climbed over rocks and through briars. Finally, William H. Blair found little Alice standing on a rock. Her clothes were in tatters, her feet red and swollen from scratches. The joyful news was shouted along the lines, "We've found her!" Strong arms soon carried her to the waiting arms of her parents, who were overcome with emotion. Alice was more than three miles from her home, deep in the thick woods. How she survived the cool nights without water or food (except for the few berries she found) was a mystery. The country for miles around rejoiced!

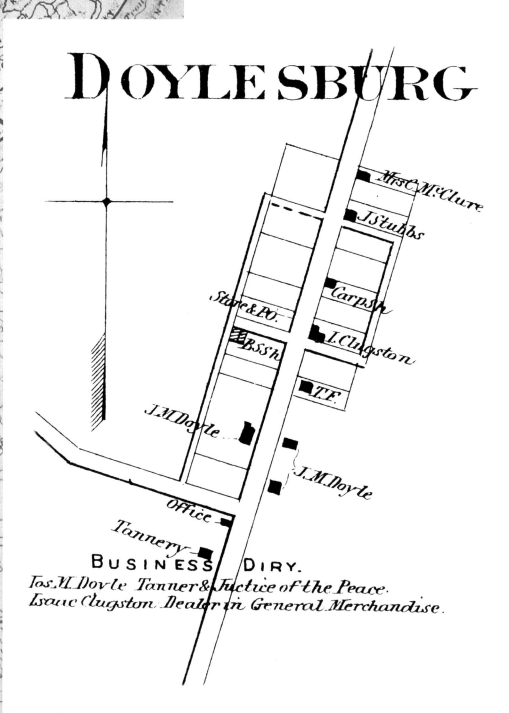

Map of Doylesburg from D. G. Beers' *Atlas of Franklin County*, 1868.

Doylestown
springhouse

The fireplace beam in this early stone house north
of Doylesburg bears the date 176? (the last digit is
indistinct). The adjoining brick house was built by the
Taylor family in the early 1800s. The family hosted
parties, weddings, and Methodist worship.

The Coulter House, north of
Doylesburg, was built between
1830 and 1840.

The farm was part of the early
Coulter tract. A natural spring in the cellar
provided refrigeration.

SPRING RUN

CHAPTER ELEVEN

*T*HE UPPER PATH VALLEY PRESBYTERIAN CHURCH, a small log structure located in the north corner of the present cemetery, formed the nucleus of Spring Run. The land warrant was procured in 1765 from John Penn and read: "Whereas, John Blair, Randall Alexander, David Elder, and James Montgomery of the county of Cumberland requested of us, that we would please to grant unto them four acres of land joining David Campbell and James Montgomery, including part of the Spring Run, in Fannett Township in the county of Cumberland, for a meeting house of religious worship." The request was affirmed on June 21, 1765, although the survey was not made until June 9, 1768. James Montgomery's land was adjacent to the tract. Organizing elders were David Elder, John Holliday, Randall Alexander and Samuel Morris.

Rev. Samuel Dougal was installed on October 9, 1775 and served both Upper and Lower Path Valley Presbyterian churches and for a time the Upper Tuscarora Church. Unfortunately, his ministry came to an abrupt end in October 1790, when he was stricken "with a severe cold which settled in his lungs," and he died. Rev. Denny was installed two years later in 1793 and served for six years. Following Denny was Rev. Amos McGinley whose ministry is described elsewhere; he arrived and served between 1802 and 1851. During this period of time, the following elders served from 1808 to 1851: James Alexander, William Alexander, John Elder, John Holliday (son of one of the first elders), Andrew Morrow, David Riddle, Stephen Skinner, James McCurdy, Sr., James McCurdy, Jr., James Dougal, John Alexander, Jacob Shearer, Peter Shearer and James Stark.

The Upper Path Valley Presbyterian Church was outgrowing its humble beginnings. A stone church was built in 1816 on the east side of the road. In 1856, it was replaced by a brick church. The art of brick making seemed to erupt in this era and new church projects prior to and during the Civil War period used brick for building in Concord, Fannettsburg, and Doylesburg. Some of the bricks used in the Presbyterian Church came from Frank Stewart's store which had been torn down.

During these years, the Upper Path Valley Presbyterian Church was not only growing in number but sending out members to minister elsewhere. As an example, F. A. Shearer born in Path Valley on January 1, 1812, felt called as a young man to become a minister. After a period of time working as a fuller at his father's mill in Amberson, he made his decision. He and his cousin Matthew started out on foot for Jefferson College on June 9, 1831. It was a "warm day and the young men soon blistered their feet. They bought a gill of whiskey which they poured into their shoes. This, he said, was the only liquor he ever bought. After a journey of two weeks they arrived at the college footsore and weary, feeling they were strangers in a strange land." After graduating from Jefferson and Allegheny Theological Seminary, Shearer studied under Rev. McGinley. In time, he mounted "the little pony given him by his father and started on his journey westward trusting the Lord to lead him to a field of labor." Having lived a long and fruitful life serving thirteen churches, Rev. Shearer died in 1905.

While the Presbyterians flourished, a second church was founded. A number of families from Germany who had originally settled in Lancaster began to arrive and mingle with the Scots-Irish. Among them were the Hammond, Kleppinger, Traxler, and Bair families. David Bair, born in 1796 in Lancaster, took up a land grant that included part of Spring Run and contained what was known as the Frank Crouse farm. A man of strong faith, Bair started the first Bible class of the United Brethren in Christ in 1830. Others date the event several years later. The meetings were held in his barn and conducted in German.

In 1814, Bair donated land for a church building. The one room edifice was built of brick and cost $506.94. Hand-hewn pews and pulpit furniture graced the interior. The church was served by David Bair and itinerant ministers. After a life of serving God and his church, David Bair died on February 27, 1844 and was buried in the Old Dutch cemetery, now part of the Upper Path Valley cemetery.

As Rev. Gordon once said in an address, "Whether Scotch-Irish or German these sturdy pioneers were Protestants and followers of the great Reformation which had revolutionized northern Europe...These two kindred streams which arose from the same general source in Europe... have flowed peacefully side by side through the generations down through this valley."

From the time of the Indians, the large spring-fed ponds and rushing creeks attracted settlers. One of the earliest homes, once owned by the Bair's and now by Dorothy Piper Medill, is located over a spring beside the creek at what is now the crossroad of old Route 75 and Route 641. A log cabin with a walk-in fireplace is incorporated in the two-story frame house. The southern section was added during the era of the Civil War.

As early as 1784 or even earlier, James Montgomery built a beautiful stone house adjacent to the Presbyterian Church. It was nestled into a bank to protect it from the westerly wind. It faced east to catch the early rays of the warming sun and an overhanging balcony on the second floor caught the cooling breezes of summer. There were fireplaces both upstairs and down. Leather straps were used to open doors. The original windows and doors were still in use in the twentieth century. The building, home of Rev. and Mrs. Clyde Brown for many years, was largely untouched by time and featured many unique characteristics.

Stone structures often required years to build, and Spring Run has a number of examples – the Hammond house adjacent to the Path Valley Restaurant and the house on the southern edge of town belonging to the Bair family and then the Crouse family. Knowledge of the characteristics of the rock at hand and finding a supply that could be cut and shaped was the first step. Shaping each stone to build a wall of firmly-fitting stones was challenging and required skill as well as infinite patience. To build a single-story house was a challenge, but to lay stones for a second floor required raw courage. A ramp was devised by which a wheelbarrow transported stones for the second floor where men used every device they had to maintain stability.

One interesting feature in the Bair/Crouse stone house was a second floor bedroom with only one exit. The stairwell opened into the kitchen, the focal point of all family activity, where an exit could not be made unobserved. As one wise historian pointed out, "It was a safeguard to prevent a young person from escaping to participate in some wild event."

According to one account, that did not stop a brave young lady from throwing her clothes out of a second floor window and making a precarious descent into the arms of her waiting lover. They rode off in haste to pledge their troth and presumably lived "happily ever after," love being stronger than the impediments placed in the structure of the house.

Education, whether sacred or secular, was part of the history of Spring Run. The Spring Run Academy, which opened about 1859, was founded by Professor Fleming in the old stone Presbyterian Church. A few years later, Professor Cyrus Madden and his sister, Sue Madby, opened a new academy located in the building behind the present brick school house. Apparently, Miss Madby and J. M. Morrison ran a boarding school in conjunction with the day school. The Academy produced strong leaders, as indicated by the fact that thirteen members in one class all became professionals. Dr. Wolk, Dr. I. Stewart, and Dr. Samuel Coons were among the graduates.

At one time in his life, Dr. Coons who lived on a farm above Dry Run had proved to be a reluctant scholar. He expressed his longing to stay home one day. His father wisely said little but sent him out to plow a rough hillside. Samuel's feet were not the strongest. In fact, some unkindly called him a cripple. After spending the day behind the plow, Samuel was glad to return to school and became an avid scholar. Later, he was a well-loved physician in Path Valley. Many who remember his kind and jovial spirit are grateful for "the plowing lesson."

The public school was filled with creative students, some of whom found that procuring a bucket of water from the spring could appreciably shorten study time. One day a fish was found in the bucket; on another day a frog. This, of course, required another trip to the spring to release the victim and return with clean water.

Spring Run was located at an important crossroad and boasted one of the area's earliest post offices. There would soon be a tannery, a flax mill, stores, and "Doc" Nesbit's blacksmith shop located under a spreading maple tree where children liked to watch the water meet the hot metal when he was forging. Every town had its shoemaker. As Clyde Crouse remembered, "Shoes hurt when they were new and when they were old. When they got wet, they stiffened up, and if you tried to dry them near a stove, they shriveled up." Meanwhile, wagons rolled up and down the roads as farms sent their produce to the cities.

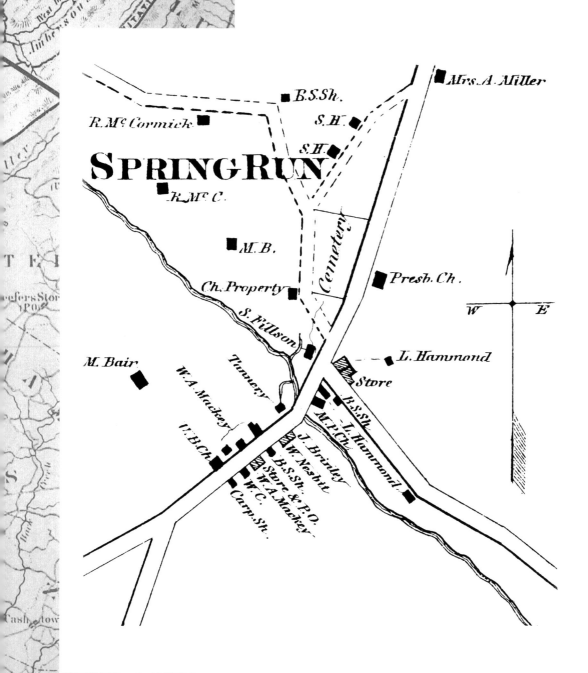

Map of Spring Run from
D. G. Beers' *Atlas of Franklin
County*, 1868.

The early Hammond property
east of Spring Run

An original cabin, built in 1764 and
embedded in this structure, may be the
first house in Spring Run.

The James Montgomery House,
west of Spring Run, was where elders
met to organize the
Presbyterian Church in 1768.

This early Bair
home, located on
the southwest side of
Spring Run, was
later known as the
Crouse farm.

MORROWTOWN

(NOW DRY RUN)

CHAPTER TWELVE

O NE OF THE EARLIEST STRUCTURES mentioned on the site that was to become Dry Run was Baker's Fort, located near the present quarry. In all likelihood, it was a fortified log house equipped with portholes from which to fire upon an enemy.

Large tracts of land were settled by the Elder, Blair, Holliday, and Alexander families. James Elder, brother of John the well-known pastor at Paxtang, received his land warrant on April 16, 1763. Reynold Alexander appeared before Governor John Penn to receive his charter in 1750. John Blair came to Path Valley in 1756.

It was not until 1838 that Dry Run, formerly Morrowtown, was founded by Stephen Skinner, who had resided in Franklin County since 1788. His son, David, born in 1815 drove a team to Pittsburgh for a number of years. In 1844, a short time after Dry Run was founded, he was able to buy three farms for $700! Davison Filson, Daniel Johnson, James Ferguson, James Stark, and Thomas Wilson settled shortly after 1838.

The James Holliday stone house was built in 1833, although others claim there was a log house on the site as early as 1783. The Hollidays arrived in 1769, the same year John was born. John married Elizabeth Coulter in 1792, became an elder in the Upper Path Valley Presbyterian Church, and represented his county in the legislature. Although some members of the family moved farther west and founded Hollidaysburg, Samuel returned to the Holliday farm and married Elizabeth McElhenny, daughter of William.

In 1836, a second house was built by James Stark who was born in Morristown, New Jersey. He was only six when his father died in 1750. His mother returned to Path Valley and bought the farm owned by Daniel Skinner. Unfortunately, James was only fourteen when his mother died, leaving him and his younger brother and sisters orphans.

The young Stark family lived in a log house with a puncheon floor and clapboard roof. James often woke up in the morning to find his blankets and his head covered with snow. In spite of the hard work required of him, James was aware of the importance of education and was determined to succeed. Gathering pine knots to stoke the fire, he studied at night while his sisters spun. James earned his first fifty cents by carrying wheat to the mill for a neighbor. By his fourteenth birthday, he had saved $5 and felt as though his fortune had been made. Before he was twenty, James had learned the miller's trade and was in charge of the mill at Orbisonia.

During Rev. McGinley's ministry, James was chosen ruling elder of the Upper Path Valley Presbyterian Church. He often helped the poor and needy and visited the sick and the lonely. Known for his ability to promote peace, he was frequently called upon to settle differences among people in the community. In 1836, James built a sturdy brick house, which replaced the log structure. At that time, only pastures and woods surrounded the Holliday and Stark houses.

A few years later, the Skinner family built the third house located at the intersection of Baltimore and Main streets. These three houses were the nucleus of the future Morrowtown.

The Elder house was located on the back road between Dry Run and Spring Run. Built of the finest stone and sporting a double porch, the Elder house was perched on a high spot overlooking the valley with views to both the north and south. It had two stairways. One led, as was the custom, to the servants' quarters over the kitchen. In the afternoon, as etiquette dictated, one girl was always dressed and ready to receive company in the parlor. The fire was lit when the sound of a buggy was heard in the distance, a signal that sent other members of the family scampering to change clothes and join their hostess in the parlor. All was ready when the guests arrived, as if the entire family had spent hours preparing for the event.

The Elder family is associated with the story of Sophia Claridge who left her home in England and sold herself to a ship's captain for her passage across the Atlantic. The vessel landed in Baltimore where Robert Elder paid the fee required for an indentured servant and brought her home to live with his mother who had five sons and no daughters.

At first, eighteen-year-old Sophia pretended to be unable to read or write. Mrs. Elder instructed one of her sons to teach her. While she pretended to be dull and incapable of learning, the boy reading the Bible to her mispronounced a word. She corrected him. "How do you know when you can't read?" he demanded. "Give me the book and I'll show you!" she retorted. With certainty and without stumbling, she read the entire chapter!

In reality, she was well educated and came to be known as "the Mistress." On her sampler she embroidered, "*Sophia Claridge is my name. Old England is my station. London is my native place, and Christ is my Salvation.*"

Sophia became a school teacher and for many years as a teacher boarded with families in the neighborhood. It was her custom to catechize and instruct both young people and their elders in the homes where she boarded. It was said that "everyone received advice they sometimes did not want, but she constantly tried to instill good manners and morals." She lived to old age and was known as "Old Sophy" or the "English lady of strong mind and determined will." Described as being slightly eccentric, her past remained a mystery, but she left an indelible stamp on those who knew her.

Her final home was in a cabin located between the Center Schoolhouse and Rev. McGinley's home.

The "Mistress" was not the only indentured servant to live in Path Valley. Peter Coons from Brunswig, Germany fought in the Revolution as part of the Regiment of Beidenell. During the course of the war, he was captured by American forces and became a prisoner of war. An indenture of $80 was paid for his release in 1782. Like so many others, he looked at the rich land and the new country and decided his future might well be on this side of the Atlantic. He eventually found his way to Path Valley and settled in the area around Dry Run. Peter was a colorful character. In his Bible was written this note, "This book is the property of Peter Coons. Steal not this book my honest friend for fear the gallows be your end." Also found in his Bible was a treasured prescription for worm medicine.

Peter died in 1808, his wife Margaret in 1820. They had seven children: Peter, George, Martin, Mary, Margaret, Barbara, and Jacob. Peter, the younger, served as the executor of his mother's estate, and William McCartney the "vendor and administrator." A bill of sale reveals the names of those who lived in the area and the amount paid for the various articles. Space does not allow a complete list, but names of the buyers are familiar to this day. George and Eleanor Coons bought "one old red cow, one stew kettle, one dish and plate, one churn and bucket," etc. William M. McCartney bought "a spinning wheel, an old wagon tire, table and band box." Samuel Bear (Bair?) purchased the log of flax. John Bear bought "one brewing tub, one can and two old vessels, one maul mattock and iron wedge." Robert Elliott purchased "ten plates and one dish, two crocks, four bowls, and a coverlet." Steven Skinner bought "livestock: two hogs; first choice, two second choice hogs, and three calves." The descriptions of cows are interesting: one spotted cow, one cow with bell, one red cow, one black-sided cow, one brown-sided cow, one red-mooly cow, and one young red and white cow.

According to scraps of local history, there were several attempts to establish churches in Dry Run. Land was given by Samuel Holliday to establish a Methodist church, but it failed. The United Presbyterians organized in 1810 and in 1822 built a stone church. James Wilson, David Ferguson, James Little, and William Robertson were the elders in charge. James Brown served as pastor. This church also failed.

A Presbyterian Sunday school sponsored by the Upper Path Valley Presbyterian Church was started in 1829 by Mrs. McGinley, Rev. McGinley's wife. Assisted by "the Mistress," sessions were held on Sunday afternoons in one-room school houses in the area: Dry Run, Hays, Mt. Joy, Ryders, Willow Hill, Wolf and Quay schools. The Dry Run Sunday school flourished.

The citizens of Dry Run slowly laid a foundation which later would make it a commercial center in Path Valley. John Coons came to Dry Run with Thomas Skinner at the age of sixteen and learned the tailor's trade. In 1854 he joined James Ferguson in the merchandising business which also included a millinery shop run by Effie Piper. There was also a coach maker in Dry Run by the name of Piper. The names Brant, Johnson, Crouse, Alexander, Doyle, Stark, Wilson, Campbell, and Flickinger were all associated with the town in the early years.

Houses were added. A descendant of Peter Coons built a handsome red brick house at the north end of town near the Skinner farm. The Ferguson house and store were in the middle of the town, but these no longer exist.

Exactly when Morrowtown became Dry Run is not known. With the Civil War looming, Dry Run, like other towns in Path Valley became a hotbed of discussion. Stores and the post office were meeting places for talk, debates, and angry comments. A war was soon to be fought and changes were coming at a rapid rate.

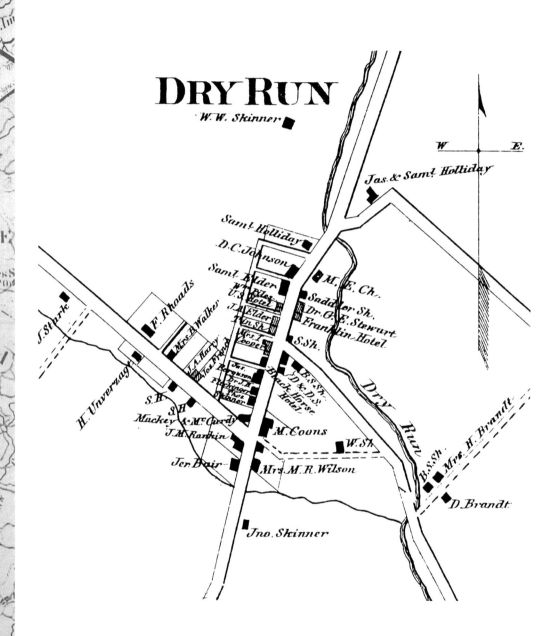

Map of Dry Run from D. G. Beers'
Atlas of Franklin County, 1868.

The Elder House was located on
Dry Run Road South near the
Zeigler farm (now Gamble farm).

This early stone house on Dry Run Road
South was built on the Alexander tract,
acquired in 1766.

The Holliday House, on the point
in Dry Run, was one of the
earliest in Dry Run.

The Skinner property on the
south side of Dry Run.

The widow Stark and her children lived in a
log cabin on this property
on Baltimore Street in Dry Run.

CIVIL WAR

CHAPTER THIRTEEN

*I*NTERNAL FORCES WERE AT WORK as the clouds of the Civil War appeared on the horizon. Locally, division was reflected at the Tuscarora Academy in Academia, where many students were from the South and friendships stretched across geographical barriers. Quietly, some of the southern students were called home by those who read the signs of the times. Later, friends would meet on the battlefield facing one another in the smoke of battle. Often, blood brothers fought on opposite sides in the fray. President Buchanan, friend and neighbor to some who lived in Path Valley, struggled to hold the nation together and hold war at bay.

North and South were deeply divided on many issues. The North had become industrialized, attracting emigrants, growing steadily in technical skill and desired an efficient banking system and internal improvements. Above all, most were against the institution of slavery. The South, on the other hand, remained rural and dependent on slave labor. Some felt it was less democratic since a small segment of the population held vast holdings and wealth. As territories in the west opened and statehood became imminent, the question of their identity as slave or free became a critical issue. The issue of slavery grew in intensity when Kansas and Nebraska territories opened for settlement and the question of their status became a critical issue.

An incident in Congress revealed the volatile atmosphere. Preston Brooks of South Carolina attacked Sumner of Massachusetts at his Senate desk with his cane and inflicted such damage that Sumner was an invalid for several years. A wise New York leader said, "If the worst agitators on both sides could be packed into a stagecoach and plunged beneath the Potomac for fifteen minutes, sectional peace might be secure." Then he added sadly, "others would take their place."

Life went on as usual in Path Valley, however. Youngsters were still roaming at night and getting into mischief. In Dry Run, some boys, in spite of their parents' watchful eyes, managed to sneak out of their houses, disassemble a wagon and put the wagon parts on the roof of Mr. Skinner's barn.

The youth around Doylesburg were known for their Halloween pranks, which sometimes included girls who managed to join the boy's gangs. Toilets were pushed into the Burns Valley creek and corn thrown over porches. Some of the boys managed to sneak into the bushes to observe dances held in Burns Valley, which were not only lively, but considered sinful in the eyes of strict Presbyterians. In a short time, many of these boys would be soldiers.

Meanwhile, everyone was following the news. In Fannettsburg, the Washington Blues who had served in the War of 1812 under Samuel Dunn reorganized. Once again, signers pledged to drill and train in anticipation of being called up. J. H. Walker was elected captain and S.C. McCurdy was first lieutenant. In Blain, John Wilson gathered together a group of men called the Washington Artillery. They believed in preparedness and were ready for action. Men gathered in groups at stores and in post offices to talk over the latest news. Women listened and worried. Once in a while in the heat of passion, angry voices would express differing opinions on the impending crisis.

Underground Railroad

In the secrecy of night, guided by a light on top of Parnell Knob, runaway slaves were quietly traveling north seeking freedom and safety. There were stations on the Underground Railroad through Path Valley, running from Fort Loudon to Waterloo in Juniata County. Lucy Witherow wrote, "On a winter evening in the 1860's, a mule-drawn stick wagon turned in the lane leading to the farm of John Park in Path Valley. The cold and weary black travelers, men, women and children, were promptly brought into the house by my great-grandmother, where they were fed and warmed by the kitchen stove. During the night, bread was baked for their journey. In the morning, they departed as quietly as they had come, never to be heard from again. Who they were, where they came from and where they were going will never be known."

According to oral history, the route north ran through Amberson or Dry Run. A hiding place was available in the loft of a spring house owned by the Holliday's on the north side of Dry Run. At the foot of the Timmons Mountain, the stone house once owned by the Hammonds had a hiding place on their third floor attic. Some found their way to the Culbertson home in Amberson. Young John remembers voices in the night as he heard a stranger say to his father, "Captain, we are chasing five runaway Negroes. We have traced them to this neighborhood. Have you seen anything of them?" His father responded, "Well, Jim, if I had I would not tell you. You don't think that I would help you in your dirty business?" The runaway slaves were fed and sent on their way. They may have crossed the mountain on the road leading from Amberson to Doylesburg. Minerva (Minnie) Campbell said someone near Doylesburg provided a safe haven. The house Earl Campbell lived in at the foot of the Round Top in Burns Valley was a way station on the Underground Railroad. At one time, Earl owned a "Black Bible" with pictures of slaves dating back to this period. The Irwin (Gamble) house north of Concord included a windowless basement room which provided a hiding place. From there, it was a relatively short distance to the home of Dr. Morrison in Waterloo who transported them to Perulack. Many of the runaways were heading for Milroy where Rev. Nourse and many in his

Presbyterian congregation provided safety and helped them on their way to Williamsport for points farther north.

Other blacks made their home in Path Valley. According to one statistic, there were forty free blacks in Fannett Township and eight in Metal during the Civil War period. A number lived in the area of Mountain Green where there is an old cemetery with fifteen to twenty graves.

An elderly slave, called Old Massa, escaped from Virginia and found his way into Burns Valley where he lived with a farmer. In need of a pair of shoes, he made a rocking chair of hickory and carried it to Concord where he traded it to Mr. Johnston for a pair of buckle brogans. (Heavy work shoes)

One of the oldest women living in this area was Hezekiah Parker, who died in 1896 at the age of 126, according to the newspaper report. She had been a waitress at George Washington's second inauguration when she was twenty-four. Apparently, her master was a kindly gentleman who had given her freedom. Parker's son was a veteran of the Civil War.

Susan Patterson, who spent most of her life in Path Valley, was another well-known figure. Susan served as custodian of the Lower Path Valley Presbyterian Church and lived in a little house built for her by the congregation. She worked not only for the church, but also for families in the area until she died at the age of eighty in 1896. Apparently she was a wise woman, for her sayings were often quoted by families in the area.

For free blacks, there was constant tension as news floated into the valley of raids around Greencastle and Chambersburg where men hunted down any negro, and boldly asserted all blacks were runaway slaves. In some cases, there was unbelievable cruelty. Starved and beaten without mercy, they were dragged south and returned to their masters or sold, in return for a fee. All blacks had a price on their heads.

As early as 1780, the Pennsylvania Legislature had given some slaves their freedom, albeit with restrictions. In time, the Presbyterian Church took issue with slavery and in the early 1800's, the United Presbyterians refused to accept any slave owner as a church member. Even in the days when the Declaration of Independence was written, founders knew the issue of slavery would become troublesome in the years to come. Not all men were created "free and equal." If the institution of slavery was not allowed to exist how-ever, some southern delegates would refuse to sign the document. Jefferson, although a Virginian, said of the stalemate, "I tremble for my country when I reflect that God is just."

The auction blocks of Baltimore and Hagerstown were not a great dis-tance from Path Valley, and business often took Path Valley residents in that direction. Some may be shocked to learn that some of our freedom loving forefathers, particularly the more affluent, were slave owners. In 1796, there were five slave owners in Lower Path Valley: George Chambers, Archibald Elliott, Ephraim Harris, John McAllen, and Wilson McKibben. With their human property valued at 30 to 150 pounds, their owners took slavery for granted. In Upper Path Valley, the Holliday, Taylor, Blair, and Elder families were listed as slave owners, and others are waiting to be discovered. As noted, even Rev. Dougal owned several, whom he later freed.

Sometimes, however, sudden and disturbing insights clarified the situa-tion. Judge Maclay, in the tanning business and a resident of Fannettsburg, was elected to the legislature in 1807. He held many important positions: judge of courts, county commissioner, member of the assembly and state senate, and member of Congress. He used to relate "with some feeling" an incident that occurred during his term in Congress. While standing on the steps of the Capitol, he watched with other legislators as a gang of slaves were driven past them on the street. One stalwart fellow with brawny arms held up his clanking chains and struck up as if in derisive mockery, in a clear, strong voice, "Hail Columbia Happy Land." As Maclay said, it "made greater impact than a dozen eloquent speeches in Congress."

Our nation was not yet a century old and still suffered from many grow-ing pains. Today, Lincoln is considered one of our greatest presidents, but comments in the *Franklin Repository* look startling to us today. Bringing news of the impeding election between Lincoln and Breckinridge, Douglas and Bell, some called Lincoln a "baboon." Others said of Lincoln, "Slaves saw a living thing uglier than themselves." In the end, Lincoln won the election of 1860. With his victory, the fragile peace maintained by President Buchanan ended. Debate became action.

THE CIVIL WAR BEGINS

Fort Sumpter fell. South Carolina seceded from the Union, followed by Mississippi, Florida, Alabama, Georgia, Louisiana, and North Carolina. Issues seemed clouded. Some attributed the action to the slavery question, others to a fight over state's rights. It was said that even General Robert E. Lee was not so much in favor of slavery as for the right of his state to determine the issue. By the time Lincoln's inauguration was celebrated, there was a Confederate nation, constitution, and president. The nation was divided.

Even in Path Valley, there were divided loyalties between North and South. A Confederate flag whipped in the wind at Spring Run. In the middle of the night, young men and boys from Dry Run came out of the darkness and tore the flag from the pole. Everyone pretended innocence.

The border between North and South was only a day's travel away, and the Confederate Army was often close to Path Valley. Family relatives continued to travel back and forth. As the machinery of warfare gathered momentum, Lincoln called for 75,000 men to defend the border. Governor Curtin raised $500,000 to put the state on a war footing. It was said that only those who lived on the border could have any perception of the "severe trials and constant strain as two contending areas engaged in bloody fraternal strife."

Those who had seen the upheaval coming had taken action. Chambers Artillery was ready to go. Before too many days, Captain J. Walker and first lieutenants S. McCurdy and John Witherow from Fannettsburg, started marching toward Chambersburg with sixty men, gathering recruits as they went.

Chambersburg was quickly becoming a center of war activity. Trains ran day and night, bringing troops, horses, wagons, baggage, provisions, and ammunition. Camp Irvin, Camp Carbon on Colonel McClure's farm, Camp Givens at the fair grounds, and Camp Slifer on the east, were organized. Men quickly enlisted; at one time it was estimated that there were 8,000 servicemen in Chambersburg.

The news from the early skirmishes, which took place not far from the Capitol, was not encouraging. The cost of the Battle of Manassas, in terms of war materials lost, was estimated at $2 million, and included a third of the muskets, 10,000 rifles, and fifty pieces of artillery. It was becoming evident that the Confederate Army under General Lee was formidable.

126TH REGIMENT

Everett and McCauley appeared in Spring Run and gave fiery speeches to encourage enlistments. Many hot and heavy conversations followed as men both young and old wavered before making a commitment to serve. In the end, it was again Captain John Walker, formerly of the Washington Blues, who raised Company H in the 126th Regiment comprised of local men, and sometimes boys.

An unknown author from the regiment wrote the following:

> On the 6th of August 1862, about 35 of us young men came to Chambersburg to enlist in the 126th Regiment. We were enrolled in Co. H. and sworn into the U.S. service and arrived in Harrisburg on the ninth where we passed up the bank of the river and were there enrolled, examined, and mustered. We then encamped in Camp Curtin, where we remained a few days until the regiment was organized and officers appointed by Governor Curtin. About the 15th, we were ordered to Washington, D.C. We marched across the old foot bridge to the south side of the river where we made our first charge on a melon car. It was not very long until the car was emptied of its load and the melons that were not eaten were rolled all over the R.R. track and some down the hill into the river. Some of the boys got very sick of the melons.

The writer then added, "I for one have not eaten a melon since." They went on their way to Washington the next morning where they rested until evening.

A typed speech by an unidentified author was directed to the Epworth League, titled *Comrades and Friends of the Grand Army*. Describing his experience at Camp Curtin, as a member of the H Company, the author wrote,

We were mustered into service in Harrisburg on the bank of the river and were turned loose into Camp Curtin in the evening about sunset, with the assurance that tents and blankets would be issued to us that evening. Some of the companies did receive them but Company H did not. About 9 o'clock I walked up through the camp feeling blue and homesick, and had nowhere to lay my head, no pillow, no covering except the firmament above. Suddenly, I heard the voice of a friend who said, 'Comrade, where are you going?' I replied, 'I do not know but I do know I have no blanket, no tent, no place to lay my head but on the ground.' Dr. Jacob Trout said, 'Come in, you shall share our tent, our blankets and all the comforts we have shall be yours.' A friend in need is a friend indeed. This was my first army experience.

On the day of the Second Battle of Bull Run, the 126th, now a part of the 5th Army Corps commanded by General John Fitz Porter, marched twenty-five to thirty miles in ninety degree August weather. They never got close to the scene of battle, but one participant (Judge Stewart) thought this one of the hardest days of his army life. Their regulation caps provided no protection from the sun, and their ears were badly sunburned.

By September, Union and rebel forces were engaged at Antietam in Maryland. War was creeping closer to home. The battleground ran red with blood and the fields of corn, planted in peace, were trampled as the fight moved from one area to another. As it turned out, the 126th was not in the battle, but part of the cleanup operations, having marched twenty-six miles.

As one member described the event, "Arrived on the battlefield at day-light when the flag of truce from Gen. Robert Lee (passed) to Gen. George McClellan was received and accepted to bury the dead…The rebel army crossed to the Virginia side of the Potomac River and left their dead for us to bury. This was a trial!" President Lincoln visited the troops to lift morale.

Another Pennsylvania soldier who walked over the battlefield after the battle wrote, "No tongue can tell, no mind conceive, no pen portray the horrible sights I witnessed this morning. God grant these things may soon end and peace be restored." To this day, once a year when darkness falls, the battlefield is filled with luminaries honoring each fallen soldier. Sentries march in the night and call to our remembrance the scope of the battle.

Learning that the 126th was close to the border, friends and families persuaded Mr. Flickinger to take supplies to their loved ones. Stoves were fired and pies, bread, cakes and cookies were baked. Hams and chickens were roasted and boxes and tubs of delicacies packed. The recipients were reportedly delighted if a little homesick.

Following the battle of Antietam, in which total losses of dead and wounded numbered more than 10,000 soldiers, 400 wounded soldiers were housed in the King Street School House, Franklin Hall, and the old Academy. The court house, churches, and private homes were also used as hospitals. Called "Antietam Angels," the local women made garments, bandages, wrappers, shirts, and pillows and provided jelly, beef rounds and dried fruit.

At this time, the 21st Cavalry was formed. Several men from Path Valley were part of this small force, which included Second Lieutenant Robert Gracey Ferguson, Franklin Gamble, and James Fegan. They had the unusual task of dealing with the Molly Maguires in Schuylkill County. In 1862, in spite of the fact that coal was needed for war purposes, labor disputes arose. The "Mollies," a secret society composed mainly of coal miners who dared to stand up to the big industrialists of the day, offered resistance to officers of the law and created riots to stop the work of the colliers. In Columbia, Northumberland, Luzerne, and Carbon counties, one violent action after another took place. One miner's journal recorded fourteen murders committed in 1863 and fourteen the following year. The 21st Cavalry was sent in to quell disturbances.

JEB STUART'S VISIT

In October, as the leaves colored in the valleys, a daring Confederate raid took place. Jeb Stuart and his men suddenly appeared in Mercersburg and demanded a county map. A Southern sympathizer directed Stuart to a house that had a detailed county map hanging on the living room wall. Jeb Stuart described the episode. "Only the females appeared, who flatly refused to let me have the map, or to acknowledge they had one; so I was obliged to dismount and push by the infuriated ladies, rather rough specimens... into the sitting room where I found the map hanging on the wall...The language and looks of these were fearful, as I coolly cut the map out of its rollers and put it in my haversack." Franklin County women were not to be trifled with.

Stuart ordered that no plundering was to take place until the border was crossed, and his men could hardly wait for the fun to begin. The stolen map directed them to roads throughout Franklin County. In the fields in Green Township, farmers were threshing wheat when soldiers seemed to appear out of nowhere. Stuart remarked: "For the fun of the thing I joined in several charges and in every case was rewarded by amusing scenes." Sometimes the invaders (despite southern accents which should have given them away) claimed to be Union soldiers impressing horses. The rebels were wearing stolen uniforms of Union blue and as a result these Southerners got an ear full of complaints about the war. When their true identity was revealed, they were rewarded with startled faces. It was reported that when the farmers found this theft had not been perpetrated by their own soldiers, they took their losses more graciously. It did hurt to think that their big Conestoga horses would soon be pulling Confederate artillery.

The Confederate party had roasted turkeys, hams, and rounds of beef strapped to their saddles as well as rolls and butter in their haversacks. They had found well-filled pantries and no end of good things to eat. But there were hungry families in Franklin County that night. It would take some time for them to recover.

Sweeping through the area, Stuart and his men came to a hill near Chambersburg. A small party was sent into town with a flag of truce to demand surrender. Since local authorities had fled, Stuart took possession of the town. A soldier reported, "As we rode in the people came to their doors freely and some spoke kindly." The men snatched a few hours rest in the drizzling rain and chill while Stuart occupied a house on the edge of town and slept on the floor in his wet clothes, arms buckled on for instant service. Before leaving, Stuart left his calling card by setting fire to the depot and some government stores filled with arms and supplies. Knowing McClellan's army was not far away, Stuart moved swiftly toward Gettysburg. There, he abruptly turned south toward Leesburg and made his escape.

Franklin County had lost from 1,000 to 1,200 horses. Railroads and railroad property had been destroyed, bakeries and warehouses were cleared out—but there was one thing Jeb Stuart had missed, Colonel McClure. He had hoped to make him captive.

Unknown to Stuart, however, McClure had been confronted by three Confederate soldiers in his own living room. When the town was ordered to surrender, McClure's safety as an officer lay in the hands of Hugh Logan, a Confederate soldier who recognized him and advised him to leave the area. The soldiers were all Virginians and gentlemen "of unusual intelligence and culture who had accepted his hospitality." For this reason, they did not reveal his identity. As McClure reported, "Every phase of the war was discussed with utmost freedom and candor on both sides without a single exhibition of prejudice or passion...When the bugle sounded, they bade me goodbye, thanking me for my hospitality and earnestly expressing the hope we should some time meet again under more pleasant auspices."

Although Path Valley had escaped the main thrust of the fighting, people felt vulnerable when their men were needed at home but away at war. People began to hide their silver in either cellars or in waterproof cases down wells, their store stock in caves, and they considered where they might hide their cattle if the Confederates invaded.

In December 1962, news came that the 126th regiment was in Fredericksburg. They marched on pontoon bridges across the Rappahannock River while shots and shells slammed into their ranks from rebel guns high on the other side of the river. Overhead, Captain Lowel was in his experimental balloon, trying to figure out enemy lines. With Major General Ambrose Burnside commanding, Captain Walker encouraged his troops to confront the enemy and reach the stone wall of Marye's Heights on the edge of Fredericksburg.

Caught at times, between the fire of soldiers behind them and the enemy in front, soldiers fell right and left. Some have described the battlefield as a blanket of blue, frozen in the brutal cold of damp December. The sounds of war mingled with the moans of the injured and dying while soldiers continued to fire at the enemy hidden on the heights above. Only the dead gave them cover. After nightfall, soldiers helped the wounded, but many of the wounded were beyond help. Bill Dietrich, William Burke, George Swain, Brice McLain, Robert Elliot, and Joseph Shearer were dead. Others were wounded: Colonel J. G. Elder was seriously hurt, Captain Walker shot through the right shoulder, Lieutenant Josiah Fletcher through the thigh. William Mackey, Samuel Elder, William Rhodes, Newel Stark and Jacob Reamer were also injured. As one of the company wrote, "In crossing back over the field, the balls were flying pretty thick, cutting the ground all around us. Along the fences the men were laying some places 3 and 4 thick, and I believe I could have crossed the field over which the charge was made by stepping on dead and wounded men and horses." General Hooker had said, "No prettier sight was had than the charge by the 126th Regiment," but it had taken its bloody toll. A columnist from a Cincinnati newspaper summed up the battle grimly, "It has never been possible for men to show more valor, or generals to manifest less judgment."

As the sounds and sights of battle died away, the sky changed color, shimmering with greens and reds as the northern lights put on an unbelievable show, a scene that caused opposing armies to pause in wonder. "We are all sharing this... both sides," said one general. "If God has smiled on us, then He will also smile on them."

Finally, the 126th went into winter quarters. The new enemies were diseased, cold, and hungry. Some began to dream of May when their enlistments would end, but there would be other battles to fight when spring came.

In the spring of 1863, the battle of Chancellorville took place in a tangle of deep, dense, dark trees and brush. It was an eerie place at night, and it was hard to tell friend from foe. The battle was intense and finally the woods caught fire. It was a cruel time for those trying to rescue the wounded and make their own escapes.

When it ended, John Stitt was missing in action and many were taken prisoner: Jeremiah Brindle, John Harrie, Josiah Fletcher, Nicolas Bowers,

James Gray, William Wilson, and John Coons. They were incarcerated at Belle Isle, Virginia.

Belle Isle was a comparatively small compound of thirteen acres. Its little stream was contaminated and a source of dysentery and typhoid. Plagued by mosquitoes and worms, the prisoners huddled together for warmth in winter and tried to find protection from the sun during the summer. A little cornmeal with husks ground in was their staple diet. At times, the prison was so crowded that prisoners found it difficult to find space to sleep. A hundred men died every day. In the end, it was estimated that more Northern soldiers perished in prisoner of war camps than in battle.

Dr. Peter DeWitt described the "great majority" of prisoners when released into his care, as being "in a semi-state of nudity... many partially lost their reason, forgetting even the date of their capture and everything connected with their antecedent history... Covered in vermin, extremely emaciated, they had to be cared for like infants."

More infamous was the Andersonville prison camp in Georgia. S.O. Skinner, James Wineman, and O.J. Gamble were captured at the Battle of Chickamaugua and all three died there.

Finally, the 126th arrived home, amid both rejoicing and grieving for the loss of familiar faces. They had traveled by boat up the Potomac from Warren Station, Virginia, marched through Washington and finally embarked on a train for Chambersburg. What the 126th had gone through showed on their faces and in their stride.

The parade was long. Rev. Nichols, who had served as their army chaplain for a period of time, gave the address to welcome them home. A banquet followed, and families were reunited. The long trek over the mountains and down the valley began in buggies, wagons, and carriages of various sorts, all filled with thankful people.

A few discussed a mystery that had occurred in the ranks of the 126th. A well-liked soldier named Frank Maine of Company F, from Juniata had deserted after the death of his close friend from home, William Fitzpatrick. Little did they know that after a period of time, Maine had re-enlisted in the west and was severely wounded in action. There, his identity was discovered.

Francis Maine was in fact Frances Day, the fiancée of William Fitzpatrick. Although relatively unknown, she represented a number of women who served in the capacity of soldier or spy in the Civil War.

OCCUPATION

The veterans were home, but the war followed them. During June of 1863, the rebels crossed the border into Franklin County. Chambersburg became General Lee's headquarters, with Generals Early and Hill stationed in the town as well.

General Lee showed many kindnesses while headquartered in the area. In Mercersburg, a little boy drawn by the arrival of troops, gaily waved the Union flag by the side of the road, thinking these were Union soldiers. General Lee stopped, drew up his horse and saluted the flag he had once served so faithfully.

Day after day for approximately three weeks, the rebels roamed the valleys appearing unexpectedly in fields and at farm houses. Farmers were at loss to know what to do. As the harvest was ready, the horses could not be spared. Yet if they were kept on the farm, a rebel raid might take both horses and cattle.

Captain Walker called his company together to guard the top of the mountain from Fannettsburg to Strasburg. Many horses, some say around two hundred, were hidden in small, secluded Horse Valley and as many as thirty men were guarding them. It was mere chance that there was not a clash at the top of the mountain between locals and Confederates. In one case, the patrols missed each other only by several hours.

Meanwhile, people were being summoned to guard the Concord Narrows. Students at the Tuscarora academy had been drafted, but older more experienced men were also needed. Students from Penn State (at that time the Agricultural College of Pennsylvania) were guarding the pass at Shade Gap. At the same time, Parsh Nesbitt and William Flickinger were busy driving cattle into a narrow tree filled valley located northeast of Concord also called Horse Valley.

About a hundred Rebels found their way over the old pack horse trail and appeared in Amberson. Benjamin Van Scyoc was not hospitable. He regarded his horses with affection and defended them with an axe saying, "The first man that crosses the door sill is a dead man." According to the story, the Confederates didn't think it worth the effort and left. By this time, the Rebels had made off with seventeen horses in the area. Work horses, riding horses, and family pets alike were taken. Peter Stake lost two, Peter Piper two, McLaughlin two, Hiram Kilpatrick one, and the Wolf's several horses.

Apparently, Mrs. McVitty Flaut was milking when twenty Confederate cavalrymen rode in to her farm where a Mr. Stouffer had brought his horses for safe-keeping. Eight horses belonging to Stouffer and one to the Flauts' were led off down the lane, but as Mrs. Flaut said, "They weren't about to take my cow!"

In one case, the raiders had a change in heart. Mrs. Peter Stake, who lived on the Clark Craig farm, saw them take the horse and the mare with a young colt. She followed, begging them to leave the mare to take care of her young, and finally they complied.

In the words of a writer of the day, "The Confederates were swarming like bees." One group crossed the mountain from McConnellsburg to Fannettsburg and traveled up the valley, fanning out in different directions.

Mrs. Miller had heard the Confederates were in Burnt Cabins when she bought sugar at the store that morning. Nevertheless, she was intent on baking cherry pies since her "Mister" enjoyed fresh pie. Living off the main road, she felt somewhat safe and started baking, but not before hiding the neatsfoot oil. It seems the Confederates were experiencing a shortage of shoes and were intent on acquiring the oil to maintain and preserve what leather they had. Satisfied with her preparations, she began seeding cherries. In time, the savory smell of fresh pastry filled the kitchen as she pulled the pies from the oven. Glancing up, she saw five or six Confederates coming up the lane. She instructed her little black girl, "Take the baby and hide! I don't want you taken South."

The soldiers, following the scent of baking, entered the house and admired the pies asking, "Would you mind exchanging two pies for two dollars?" They were very polite! Naturally, Mrs. Miller expressed the hope they would enjoy the pies, and they departed as Southern gentlemen would, graciously and gratefully.

Once the men were out of sight, she looked for her servant girl and the baby. They had disappeared. She was beginning to feel frantic, wondering if the Southerners had taken more than pies. Finally, she found her little black girl cowering in a dark corner of the attic, and cradling the baby.

Rebel incursions were frequent. One day at Spring Run, Mrs. Clugston was baking bread. The family had hidden their meat and supplies in the spring house and covered the entrance with corn fodder. Suddenly, the Confederates appeared, thrusting their sabers into the fresh loaves of bread as they grabbed a crock of butter. From outside the house came a triumphant shout. The hidden spring house had been found! The rebels made off with the family's entire stash of meat.

The rebels also appeared at the Elder farm outside Dry Run. Hearing the approach of horses, the women stashed the silver in their stockings beneath their voluminous skirts. The Elder women were exceedingly polite and invited the soldiers into the parlor. Instead of waiting for them to demand food, they offered it. Years later, when the house fell on hard times and was being dismantled, Confederate bills were found behind the mantel.

During one raid, soldiers ventured into Burns Valley rounding up horses and cattle. A neighbor stopped by the Coulter home and found Matthew Coulter in his cellar, frantically burying his gold.

There was at all times a sense of impending danger. One quiet summer evening, a man galloped into Concord and shouted, "The Confederate cavalry is only a few miles south of town." Determined that no rebel was going to help himself to the leather at the Harris tannery, the cannon balls at McKim's foundry, or the goods in their stores, the men hurriedly armed themselves. The women stood ready to attack the enemy with brooms, hoes and pitchforks. A man yelled, "Here they come!" and a herd of cattle appeared over the hill driven by a man trying to get them to Huntingdon County and safety. Weapons were put down and the latest information shared.

Farther down the valley, news came to Fannettsburg about a battle at Burnt Cabins between a small group of Union and Confederate soldiers. Apparently, the New York Cavalry stationed at Mt. Union surprised the Confederates and thirty-two of them were taken prisoner with the help of people from Burnt Cabins. According to one rider, the whole population rushed into the street with whatever weapons they had and pursued the Confederates, yelling at the top of their lungs.

Questions arose. How were the Confederates finding their way into these hidden valleys? It was said that a man with a mask was leading them. A traitor lived in Franklin County? Another possibility was that a Franklin County citizen had moved south, was sympathetic to the rebel cause, had returned with those forces and helped to direct their exploits.

The valley was left all but defenseless against the marauding Confederates. As someone said bitterly, "We scarce have enough men to serve as pall bearers." Most families were missing sorely needed manpower.

For three long weeks, the Confederates made their presence known. Everyone wondered when General Lee would move out of the area. The general consensus was that Harrisburg would be Lee's destination. Others optimistically hoped he would return to Virginia. Finally, the Confederates gathered and began to march toward Gettysburg.

A short time later, the sound of hoof beats was heard in Concord as Stephen Pomeroy jumped off his weary, lathered horse in front of his uncle's home. Breathlessly he asked, "May I have something to drink and eat and a fresh horse to continue my journey?" All he had time to convey was that Judge Kimmel in Chambersburg had sent a message to Governor Curtin in Harrisburg. Confederates had turned east toward Gettysburg. The papers were in the buckle strap of Pomeroy's pantaloons. He had traveled by foot seventeen miles, hiding in cornfields while fired on by Confederates. Reaching Roxbury, he found a horse and from there made his way slowly through a road blocked with trees to Amberson Valley. Crossing the mountain from Amberson to Doylesburg, he swiftly covered the miles to Concord.

After quickly eating at his uncle's house, Pomeroy galloped off through the Concord Narrows, stopping long enough to say a few words to the young men guarding the Narrows. Rumor had it that he had been killed at Chancellorsville, and the young men were relieved to see him alive. He stopped at Rev. David Beale's at Honey Grove and grabbed some food before going on to his uncle Joseph Pomeroy at Academia. Changing horses, he rode pell-mell to Port Royal, arrived at midnight, and sent the message. Governor Curtin was in his office with A. K. McClure when the dispatch arrived. Governor Curtin always maintained it was this message that saved the day at Gettysburg and turned the tide of the war. In addition to the seventeen miles Pomeroy had walked, he had ridden more than forty miles. As his aunt had said upon his arrival, "Why, Steve, is that you or your ghost? We thought you were dead."

GETTYSBURG

A few days later, people heard the sound of thunder. It was perplexing. The sky was clear and blue, but the sound persisted. Some put their ears to the ground and felt the earth vibrating. Few realized the sounds of the Battle at Gettysburg were carrying through the earth. On the second day of the battle, the temperature reached 108 degrees. Some said they saw reflections of bayonets glinting in the clouds overhead, reflecting the intensity of the battle.

Several days later, a group of young men which included George McCormick, went to Gettysburg and were sickened by what they heard, saw, and smelled. "Branches from trees and leaves were gathered for beds. Paper, shreds of clothing, photographs, muskets, ramrods, knapsacks, caps, old shoes, blankets, and dead horses littered the ground. There was the stench of death. An urgent call had gone forth for carpenters and undertakers. Boxes for the dead, a dollar apiece, were advertised. The enormity of the battle began to filter through lines of communication.

Long trains of wagons carrying the injured began the trek south. Chambersburg was filled with the ghastly aftermath of the battle. King Street Hospital overflowed with the wounded, Union and Confederate soldiers alike, who were nursed by local people. Path Valley did what it could in sending food and items such as soap and linens, even though larders in many homes were depleted. It seemed as if the earth itself was groaning in despair over these young men from both the North and the South who were injured or had lost their lives.

News came from Fannettsburg that some twenty Union soldiers coming from the west had lodged at the Fannettsburg Inn. In a drunken brawl, one was killed and hurriedly buried in a fence row near town. There was also a black Civil War soldier buried in the area of Mountain Green, his circumstances unknown.

Yet, in the midst of the cruelty of war, there were stories of kindness. Confederate soldiers were marching through one town when several observed a two-year-old boy rocking precariously close to the edge of a porch. Soldiers broke ranks to save him from falling.

Excitement mounted when the news came that President Lincoln would be in Gettysburg on November 18 to dedicate the cemetery. Some were brave enough to make the journey. The list of notables in attendance was long and the gathering impressive. The Honorable Edward Everett spoke for several hours. When President Lincoln came to the podium, people expected a long speech, but the speech he offered was brief. His stirring words had a life of their own. Soon people were reciting them by heart.

Many young men who had been part of the 126th were now re-enlisting and joining other units. A story that illustrates the fervor of their devotion to their country came through Floyd Lytle. Charlie Burk of Amberson was considered too short to fight. He solved the problem by having a pair of shoes made to give him enough height to be accepted. Fighting with the 102nd Pennsylvania Infantry, he served under General Sheridan. During a battle near Winchester, he stood behind a large white oak tree with rebel bullets cutting the bark off on each side. When General Sheridan came riding through the woods, he called, "Hello little one. What are you doing here? Come out here and give it to them. The lead that will kill me is still in the mine." A short time later, a minnie ball went through Sheridan's abdomen, but in time, he recovered. Meanwhile, Charlie Burk celebrated his fifteenth birthday in the Battle of Winchester and told his family it was the liveliest birthday he had ever had.

Many young men from Path Valley fought in the battle at Petersburg, Virginia. As part of the plan, Pennsylvania miners dug a tunnel to plant explosives underneath the Confederate fort to destroy the stronghold of the Confederates. After several attempts, "a monstrous tongue of flame shot fully two hundred feet in the air, and then a great fountain of red earth rose to a great height, mingled with men and guns, timbers and debris, all spreading, whirling and scattering." When the Union soldiers reached the huge crater, they stopped to dig Confederate survivors from the wreckage. Had they pushed to the heights beyond which was the plan, they might have captured Petersburg that day. Brotherhood reveals itself in unexpected ways. Soldiers could shoot at each other one moment but on nightly patrol exchange tobacco for coffee or exchange one newspaper for another.

A number of Path Valley soldiers participated in the Battle of Petersburg. During the siege, James Fegan was wounded and his brother-in-law, Sylvester McElheney, was killed. At the same time, Joseph McElheney was serving at Fort Stedman, a large earthwork east of Petersburg. Fighting beside his friend Charles Shields, Joseph gave Charles his watch and trinkets to take home to his wife, Harriet, when he fell in battle. Six of the nine sons of Thomas and Susanna Shields fought in the Civil War. James was killed.

BURNING OF CHAMBERSBURG

While the war went on in the South, a force under John McCausland was turning north. Chambersburg was their destination, a beautiful town with the gleaming pillars of the courthouse, gracious homes, and Colonel McClure's home with its lovely gardens and stately trees. McCausland's forces marched in and the general demanded $100,000 in gold, an amount impossible to raise. McCausland ordered the town razed.

The fire was started in the middle of town and quickly spread, destroying everything in its path. The heartlessness of some of the soldiers, unlike those under General Lee, has been reported. In one case, a soldier poured gun powder under one helpless woman's chair. An invalid for three years, she was unable to walk. As the soldier poured, he said, "This will teach you to walk." It was reported that one Southern soldier was heard to say under his breath, "General McCausland has made us all thieves and murderers." A Southern officer was seen going south in handcuffs because he had disobeyed orders. In the midst of the fire, some people took refuge in the Falling Spring cemetery. Colonel McClure's home did not escape. Although his family had nursed Southern soldiers, now they met only hatred and retaliation. It was a far cry from their experience with Stuart's officers.

Finally, seizing what booty they could, McCausland and his forces turned south, leaving parts of Chambersburg in rubble. The citizens, however, gathered for worship on Sunday and made plans for rebuilding. Again, Path Valley residents went through their houses to find extra bedding, clothing, and pots and pans, then looked for food they could share. When and where they could, they shared their skills and labor.

Petersburg, Virginia, was now in the hands of Union forces. Richmond was a picture of desolation, half burned by the Confederates themselves. As Union troops pursued Lee, they observed signs of dissolution and discouragement among their Southern counterparts. The roads were strewn with discarded tents, ammunition, Dutch ovens, and in some cases muskets were found in fence corners. On they marched toward Farmville.

PEACE

Troops camped in the fields around Appomattox Court House. Edward Flickinger of Dry Run and Major Nevins of Willow Hill were busy preparing for another battle. Unfortunately, in a preceding skirmish, Nevins had lost his gun. Turning to Eddie, he asked for his and told him to hold both their horses. According to Flickinger, Nevins, using his gun, fired the first shot in the battle that brought lasting victory to the Union Army.

Following the battle, there came a stillness as if the world were holding its breath. Known to Union forces, General Grant was residing in the McLean house. Soldiers close enough to observe may have been surprised to see General Lee appear on his horse Traveler, dismount, and enter the house. Silence fell over the troops. "Will he surrender?" was the question that hammered in their minds. Union officers were observed saluting Lee. When surrender appeared evident, wild cheering followed until Grant sent word that the troops were not to exult over their enemy's downfall. It is one of the ironies of war that the McLean family had owned a farm overrun during the Battle of Manassas. In an attempt to elude the war they had moved to Appomattox. The treaty was signed in their house!

General Grant allowed the Confederates, who were technically prisoners of war, to keep their horses for plowing and sent them home to rebuild, an effort to turn enemies into friends. It was an awesome day, a day to give thanks for the gifts of life and hope. Lincoln made plans to heal the wounds, unlike some of his Northern cohorts who wanted to punish the South.

At home, news of the surrender trickled through lines of communication. As the news was received, church bells started to ring in succession throughout the valley, announcing the joyful news. Musket fire soon followed. Preparations for celebrations began.

When the war came to an end, the valley returned to its routine. There were empty chairs around a number of tables, however. The young had fallen at Fredericksburg, Petersburg, and Gettysburg among many other battle fronts. Many came home with their health broken from lack of food and long marches without rest, not to mention the wounds of battles. Many others had lost their lives not on the battlefield but as prisoners of war or victims of disease.

Another tragedy occurred on April 15, 1865 that would have far-reaching effects on both North and South. President Lincoln was assassinated by

John Wilkes Booth, who was described as a Southern patriot! A stunned nation recoiled, all business was suspended, and bells tolled from eleven a.m. until nightfall. Every residence, office, workshop, and place of worship in Chambersburg was draped in mourning. Dignitaries and citizens gathered. Speeches were made by C.S. Eyster and others.

Joy and sorrow! With the death of Lincoln, measures intended to heal the chasm between North and South were postponed. Sectional divisions continued, but after a long period of healing, new growth patterns carried the nation into a brighter future. Many exciting developments were taking place.

THE NAMES OF THOSE KILLED
IN THE CIVIL WAR:

FROM THE UPPER PATH VALLEY
PRESBYTERIAN CHURCH MONUMENT

2nd Pa. Heavy Artillery: William A. Gaston

28th Regiment P.V. Amos Neil

2nd Regiment P.V. Andrew McClure

202nd Reg. P.V. William P. Fegan

49th Reg. P.V. Gilbert McLain, David Wolff, George Standford

Unknown Reg. Joseph A. Piper, James Logan, Charles W. Boltz

9th Pa. Cavalry Solomon Dunkle, David H. Piper, Joseph McVitty, Smith Van Scyoc, James Shields, Matthew Seibert, Joseph W. Evitts, Ambrose Price, George W. McConley, Wilson Haynes, Jacob Shetler, Jonathan L. Shearer

21st Pa. Cavalry Franklin Gamble

149th Reg. P.V. J. Milton Gamble, Simon Neil, Conrad Holliday

126th Reg. John H. Stitt, Robert F. Elliott, William H. Rhoades, Wm. J. Harrison, Wm. H. Burke, Innes Johnson, Brice B. McLain, Joseph B. Shearer, Henry Wallace

77th Reg. P.V. Stephen O. Skinner, David B. Miller, Oliver J. Gamble, Frederick Sharp, James Wineman, James Craig

19th Pa. Cavalry James M. Wilson

158 Reg. Pa. Hugh L. Campbell, Charles Ray, Levi Line

102 2nd Pa. Jacob Piper, Hugh L. Finley, Joseph B. Mcllheny

208th Reg. Syvester W. Mcllheny

13th: John Skinner, J. Thompson Ardery

198th Reg. Robinson Craeamer, Noah H. Shearer

(Please note that spelling differences occur in names. These have been copied as they were written. Hopefully, someone will research and find where these fell in the line of duty.)

Note: Oliver Gamble, Oliver Skinner and James Wineman died in Southern prison pens. James Craig died of disease at Stone River, Tennessee. John Forsythe and Frederick Sharp died on the fever-laden shores of Green Lake, Texas.

Eleven soldiers from Juniata County died at Andersonville and three from the effects shortly after they were moved.

ADDITIONAL SOLDIERS WHO SERVED FROM AMBERSON

John W. Bankis, Samuel Crouse, Benjamin J. Culbertson, Jacob Dunkle, Sylvester J. Eckenrode, George Fogal, Simon French, William E. Funston, Nehemiah K. Harvey, Joseph M. McVitty, Stephen D. McVitty, Ezra M. Piper, L. Martin Piper, Louis S. Piper, William Piper, Sylvester Price, James Rea, Jonah E. Shearer, John Shetler, Charles S. Shields, Daniel B. Shields, George Shields, Levi Shields, Pius Shields, William A. Shields, William C. Shields, George Stanford, Franklin Taylor, Martin Taylor, Smith Van Scyoc, Gideon C. Varner, David Wolfe, John A. Wolfe, Daniel Wolff, George Wolff, Isaac Worthington, Henry Wyrick

Killed in Action: William Gaston, George Piper, Jacob Piper, Michael Piper, Ambrose Price, James Price, Joseph Rea, Hardin Shearer, Markle Shearer, James Shields, James Van Scyoc

SERVICEMEN LISTED AT THE AMERICAN LEGION MONUMENT

The following list of servicemen who survived is copied from the monument at the American Legion. In some cases, spellings differ:

William Adair, David Bair, Simon Bair, Randall Barclay, Montgomery Barnhart, P.C. Bealman, George Berrier, Isaac Bingham, John Boggs, Stewart Brackbill, Daniel Bricker, George Brininger, George Brinley, Noah Brinley, Charles Burk, John Campbell, Boyd Clendeming, David Clippinger, Howard Clugston, Melchoir Concord, William Cook, John Coons, Peter G. Coons, Peter Coons, Henry Crouse, John Crouse, Samuel Crouse, James Culbertson, John Culbertson, Robert Davis, G. Dawney, Hezekiah Dayton, Amos Devor, Simon Devor, Henry Doyle, John Doyle, George Dunkle, Sylvester Eckenrode, Hezekiah Edmonson, G.W. Erninbizer, James Fegan, Thomas Fegan, David Ferguson, Gracey Ferguson, William Finney, Samuel Fleming, Edgar Flickinger, J. Chambers Flickinger, James Fogal, Joel Frederick, Joseph French, Simon French, Solomon French, William French, Charles Friend, John Fulton, William Funston, Carl Gallagher, Samuel Gamble, Frederick Camp, Alex Gaston, William Gaston, William Giles, Gordon Frank, George Goshorn, David Gracey, Isaac Groce, Isaiah Guyer, Jacob Guyer, Allen Haiston, Mercer Haiston, Equilla Hancock, James Hancock, John Hancock, Solomon Hancock, John Harry, Titus Harry, Jacob Hartmeir, Joseph Harvey, Cyrus Hazlett, Thomas Heater, Albert Heckman, John Henderson, W.A. Hinchman, Alex Hockenberry, Isaac Hockenberry, William Hockenberry, Wilson Hockenberry, Thomas Horton, Isaac Houck, Hexekiah Huffmaster, John Irwin, J.W.C. Irwin, Samuel Johns, Samuel Johnston, Brook Jones, David Jones, John Jones, Samuel Jones, Sylvester Jones, John Keasey, James Kegerreis, Michael Kegerreis, James Kell, James Kelly, Job Kennedy, Alford Kent, Robert Kerr, Elisha Kling, Job Lacy, Jacob Leedy, Joseph Lessig, John Lewis, A.E. Linn, George Linn, David Mason, John Mason, William Maclay, R.W. McAllen,

Gibert McClain, Anthony McCurdy, J.A. McCurdy, Oliver McCurdy, Phillip McElheny, George McGowan, James McGowan, David McKelvey, Edward McVitty, Steven McVitty, D.F. Miller, James Miller, J.C. Miller, John Mohn, Edward Moore, J.M. Moore, Allen Mot, William Mort, George Murry, Daniel Mutersbaugh, George Needham, John A. Neil, John J. Neil, Michael Neil, John Newlin, John Nimmon, William Noble, Peter North, Alexander O'Donnel, Alex Orr, Hezekiah Parker, E. Piper, Jonathan Piper, Lewis Piper, Mark Piper, William Piper, Wilson Piper, John Piles, P.G. Piles, P.J. Piles, Sylvester Price, George Reed, John Reeder, J.F. Rhodes, Isaac Richardson, John Rodeniser, Abraham Rosenberry, John Rowels, John Russell, Richard Sanders, William Seibert, John Shaffer, William Shaffer, Adam Sharpe, Matthew Sharpe, William Sharpe, Amos Sharpe, A. Shearer, J.M. Shearer, Jonah Shearer, Samuel Shearer, John Shetler, Charles Shields, Daniel Shields, David Shields, George Shields, Pius Shields, William Shields, C. M. Skinner, Edgar Skinner, Ezra Skinner, John Skinner, William Speck, Daniel Smith, John Smith, Peter Smith, David Snyder, James Standford, Valentine Steck, Samuel St. Clair, David Steward, Simon Stewart, W. Stringer, Frank Taylor, Marlin Taylor, John Thomas, John Tilley, Benjamin Van Scoyc (Scyoc), John Scoyc, Samuel Scoyc, Gideon Varner, Noah Varner, Wilson Varner, John Walker, Solomon Warnick, John West, Jacob Wilheim, John Wilheim, McGinly Wilheim, John Wilson, Joseph Wilson, Matthew Wilson, Matthew C. Wilson, George Wineman, J. H. Witherow, William Witherow, Samuel Witter, Daniel Wolff, George Wolff, John Wolff, Thomas Woods, James Worthington, Henry Wright, Henry Wyrick, Jacob Zeigler, Daniel Zimmerman

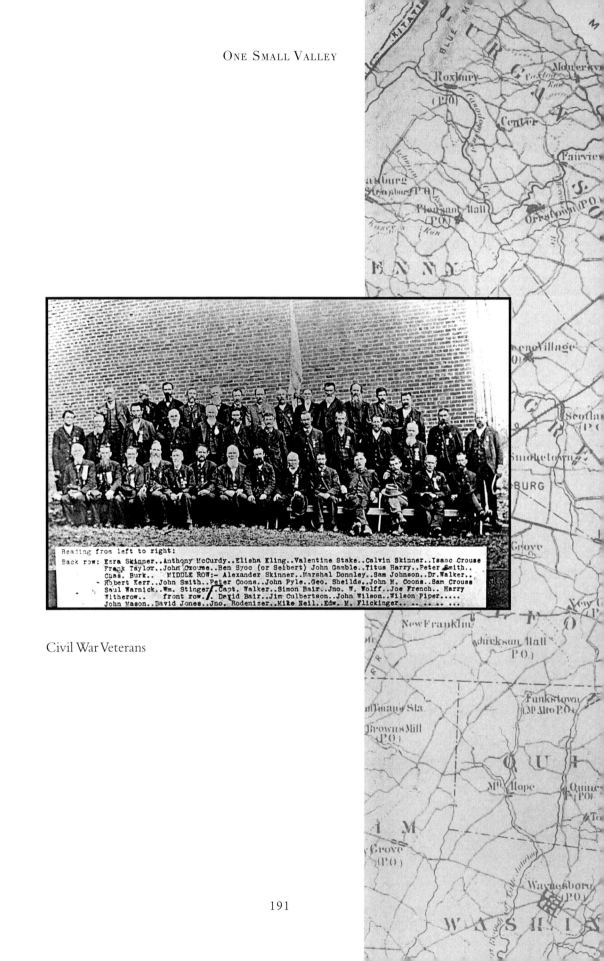

Reading from left to right:
Back row: Ezra Skinner..Anthony McCurdy..Elisha Kling..Valentine Stake..Calvin Skinner..Isaac Crouse
   Frank Taylor..John Crouse..Ben Syoc (or Seibert) John Gamble..Titus Harry..Peter Smith..
   Chas. Burk..   MIDDLE ROW:- Alexander Skinner..Marshal Donnley..Sam Johnson..Dr.Walker..
   Robert Kerr..John Smith..Peter Coons..John Pyle..Geo. Sheilds..John M. Coons..Sam Crouse
   Saul Warnick..Wm. Stinger..Capt. Walker..Simon Bair..Jno. W. Wolff..Joe French.. Harry
   Witherow..   front row:/. David Bair..Jim Culbertson..John Wilson..Wilson Piper.....
   John Mason..David Jones..Jno. Rodenizer..Mike Neil..Edw. M. Flickinger.. .. ..

Civil War Veterans

ABOUT THE AUTHOR

ALICE MCFEELY MELOY earned her undergraduate degree from Penn State, followed by a M.Div. from Princeton Theological Seminary. She is a retired Presbyterian (PC-USA) pastor who has served churches in the Philadelphia area and central Pennsylvania. She has also written a variety of devotional and historical articles, and a number of historical scripts, including scripts for New Jersey Public Television. Alice's maternal roots are in Path Valley. She has been gathering stories of the Valley since she was a teenager, and is grateful for the family and friends who have shared their stories, their faith, and their adventures. The history has been a labor of love.

BIBLIOGRAPHY

CHAPTER ONE

Dunaway, Wayland F. *The Scotch-Irish of Colonial Pennsylvania*. Chapel Hill, NC: The University of North Carolina Press, 1944.

Eastman, Charles A. *The Soul of the Indian*. Lincoln, NE: University of Nebraska Press, 1980.

Harrington, Mark R. *The Iroquois Trail*. New Brunswick, NJ: Rutgers University Press, 1965.

Jordan, John. *History of the Juniata Valley and Its People*. New York: Lewis Historical Publishing Co., 1913.

Lawson, John. *The History of Carolina*. London: John Stevens, 1711.

Leyburn, James G. *The Scotch-Irish: A Social History*. Chapel Hill, NC: The University of North Carolina Press, 1962.

McLuhan, Terry C. *Touch the Earth*. New York: Promontory Press, 1971.

Nerburn, Kent, and Louise Mengelkoch. *Native American Wisdom*. Novato, CA: The Classic Wisdom Collection New World Library, 1991.

Palmer, Rose A. *The North American Indians*. New York: Smithsonian Institution, 1929.

Sipes, Hale C. *The Indian Wars of Pennsylvania*. Harrisburg, PA: Telegraph Press, 1929.

CHAPTER TWO

Bates, Samuel P. *History of Franklin County, Pennsylvania.* Chicago: Warner, Beers and Company, 1887.

Foreman, Harry E. *Forbes Road: Parnell's Knob to Burnt Cabins.* Chambersburg, PA: Privately printed, 1954.

Hunter, William A. *Forts on the Pennsylvania Frontier, 1753-1758.* Harrisburg, PA: The Pennsylvania Historical and Museum Commission, 1960.

Jones, U. J. *History of the Early Settlement of the Juniata Valley.* Harrisburg, PA: Telegraph Press, 1940.

O'Meara, Walter. *Guns at the Fork.* Pittsburgh, PA: Pittsburgh University Press, 1979.

Sipes, C. Hale. *Indian Wars of Pennsylvania.*

Wallace, Paul A. W. *Indians in Pennsylvania.* Harrisburg, PA: The Pennsylvania Historical and Museum Commission, 1964.

———. *Pennsylvania: Seed of a Nation.* New York: Harper and Row, 1962.

CHAPTER THREE

Hughes, Daniel L. *A Sketch of the Life, Character, and Writings of the Reverend James Y. M'Ginnes of Shade Gap, Pa.* Philadelphia: Joseph M. Wilson, 1854.

Kelly, Joseph. *Pennsylvania, the Colonial Years, 1681–1776.* New York: Doubleday and Co., 1980.

Langdon, William C. *Everyday Things in American Life, 1607–1776.* New York: Charles Scribner's Sons, 1943.

Leyburn, James C. *The Scotch-Irish: A Social History.*

Metzler, Mary. *Shade Gap Area Centennial.* Privately printed, 1971.

Stevenson, Fletcher W. *Pennsylvania Agriculture and Country Life, Volume I (1640–1840).* Harrisburg, PA: Pennsylvania Historical and Museum Commission, 1971.

Weslager, Clinton A. *Magic Medicines of the Indians.* Somerset, NJ: The Middle Atlantic Press, 1962.

CHAPTER FOUR

Albion, Robert G., and Leonidas Dodson. *Philip Vickers Fithian: Journal 1775–1776.* Princeton, NJ: Princeton University Press, 1934.

Camp, D. I., and Warren Kaufman. *History of the Presbyterian Churches of Path Valley: Addresses Delivered at the Sesquicentennial of the Upper and Lower Path Valley Churches and a History of These Churches.* Chambersburg, PA: Chambersburg Repository, 1916.

Fariah, Hunter D. *Journals and Letters of Philip Vickers Fithian, 1773–1774.* Williamsburg, VA: Colonial Williamsburg, Inc., 1965.

Klett, Guy S. *Journals of Charles Beatty, 1762–1769.* University Park, PA: Pennsylvania University Press, 1962.

———. *Minutes of the Presbyterian Church in America, 1706–1788.* Philadelphia: Presbyterian Historical Society, 1976.

McClure, Millie Beale, and Eleanor Work. *History of the Middle Tuscarora Presbyterian Church, 1776–1779.* Privately printed, [1942].

Nevin, Alfred. *Churches of the Valley.* Philadelphia: Joseph Wilson, 1852.

Presbytery of Carlisle. *Centennial Memorial of Carlisle Presbytery: Volume I.* Harrisburg, PA: Meyers Publishing and Printing House, 1889.

Chapter Five

Bates, Samuel P. *History of Franklin County, Pennsylvania.* Evansville, IN: Unigraphic, Inc., 1975. First published 1887.

Benchoff, Lucy C. F. *The Courageous Women of the Valley.* Mercersburg, PA: Kittochtinny Historical Society, Volume XVI, 1977.

Bowen, Catherine Drinker. *Miracle at Philadelphia.* Boston: Little, Brown and Co., 1986.

Crouse, Dorothy. *Peter Coons and Descendants, 1782–1980.* Privately printed.

Fendrick, Virginia Shannon. *American Revolutionary Soldiers of Franklin County.* Chambersburg, PA: Daughters of the American Revolution (Historical Works Committee of the Franklin County Chapter), 1969.

Ketchum, Richard M. *Saratoga: Turning Point of American's Revolutionary War.* New York: Henry Holt and Co., 1997.

Lancaster, Bruce, and J. H. Plumb. *The American Heritage Book of the Revolution.* New York: American Heritage Publishing Company, 1958.

Langguth, A. J. *Patriots: The Men Who Started the American Revolution.* New York: Simon and Schuster, 1988.

Linn, John Blair, William Egle, and Clarence M. Busch. *Pennsylvania in the Revolution, Volumes I and II.* Harrisburg, PA: State Printer of Pennsylvania, Clarence Busch, 1895.

McDowell, Bart. *The Revolutionary War.* Washington, DC: National Geographic Society, 1967.

McCullough, David. *1776.* New York: Simon and Schuster, 2005.

Nevins, Allan, and Henry St. Commager. *A Short History of the United States.* New York: Modern Library, 1956.

Ramsey, David, and Lester H. Cohen. *The History of American Revolution, Volumes I and II.* Indianapolis, IN: Liberty Fund, Inc., 1990.

Schlesinger, Arthur M. *The Almanac of American History.* New York: Putnam, 1983.

Shearer, Fred W. *The Colonial Military Organization of Lower Path Valley.* Mercersburg, PA: Kittochinny Historical Society, Volume XVI, 1978.

Smith, James. *An Account of the Remarkable Occurrences in the Life and Travels of Colonel James Smith, Written by Himself.* Lexington, MA: John Bradford on Main Street, 1799.

St. Clair, Arthur. "Second Pennsylvania Battalion," Pennsylvania State Archives, Harrisburg, vol. 2, series 5 (January 1776–January 1777).

Stevens, Sylvester K. *Pennsylvania: Birthplace of a Nation.* New York: Random House, 1964.

Swanson, Neil H. *The First Rebel.* New York: Farrar and Rinehart, 1937.

Thatcher, James. *Military Journal of the Revolution.* Hartford, CT: William Hurlbut and Co., 1862.

Trussell, John B. B. *The Pennsylvania Line Regimental Organization and Operations, 1776–1783.* Harrisburg, PA: Pennsylvania Historical Museum Commission, 1977.

Webb, James. *Born Fighting: How the Scots-Irish Shaped America.* New York: Broadway Books, 2004.

CHAPTER SIX

Dwight, Margaret Van Horn. *A Journey to Ohio in 1810.* New Haven, CT: Yale University Press, 1912.

Gibson, William J. *History of Huntingdon Presbytery, 1795–1895.* Bellefonte, PA: Bellfonte Press, 1874.

Godcharles, Frederic A. *Daily Stories of Pennsylvania.* Milton, PA: privately printed, 1924.

Goodyear, B. R. *Wagons and Wagoners of 1840.* Chambersburg, PA: Kittochtinny Historical Society, Volume III. Kerr Printing, 1901.

Hastings, Sally. "1800 Diary," *The Public Opinion,* April 24, 1970.

Hulbert, Archer Butler, and Dorothy Printup. *Across Land and Sea to Oregon, Volume 5.* Denver, CO: Colorado College, Stewart Commission, 1935.

Lewis, David. *The Confessions and Narrative of David Lewis.* Carlisle, PA: privately printed, 1820.

Orr, John. *Whiskey Rebellion: General Washington's Journey to Bedford.* Chambersburg, PA: Kittochtinny Historical Society, Volume I, 1899.

Shearer, Fred. *The Origin of a Church: The Lower Path Valley Presbyterian Church.* Chambersburg, PA: Kittochtinny Historical Society, Volume XV, Kerr Printing Company, 1970.

Unger, Frederick Fleming. *Old Bridges of Franklin County.* Franklin County, PA: Seilhammer, Rupp, and Beers, 1941.

CHAPTER SEVEN

Bates, Samuel. *History of Franklin County,* 1887.

Benn, Carl. *The Iroquois in the War of 1812.* Toronto, Ontario: University of Toronto Press, 1953.

Jones, U. J. *History of the Early Settlement of the Juniata Valley.* Harrisburg, PA: Telegraph Press, 1940.

Mahon, John K. *The War of 1812.* New York: Da Capo Press, 1972.

Nevins, Allan, and Henry Commager. *A Short History of the United States.* New York: Modern Library, 1956.

Shearer, Fred. *The Lower Path Valley Presbyterian Church During the Ministry of Reverend A. McGinley.* Chambersburg, PA: Kittochtinny Historical Society, Volume XVI, Kerr Printing Company, 1978.

CHAPTER EIGHT

Bates, Samuel. *History of Franklin County,* 1887.

Beers, D. G. *Atlas of Franklin County, Pennsylvania.* Philadelphia: Pomeroy and Beers, 1868.

Burgner, Milton. *Carrick Furnace.* Chambersburg, PA: Kittochtinny Historical Society, Volume XI, 1937.

Camp, D. I., and J. Warren Kaufman. *History of Path Valley Presbyterian Churches.* Chambersburg, PA: Chambersburg Repository, 1916.

Chilcote, Bess, and Clair Hammond. *The Presbyterian Churches of Path Valley: Amberson 1766–1966.* Shippensburg, PA: Beidel Printing House, 1966.

Crider, Doris Campbell. Interviews with Alice M. Meloy, 1976–2011.

Foreman, Harry E. *The Skinner Inns from Conodoguinet Secrets.* Chambersburg, PA: Kittochinny Historical Society, Volume XIII, Kerr Printing Company, 1957.

Lower Path Valley Presbyterian Church Cookbook (1793–1993). Fannettsburg, PA: privately printed, 1994.

McAllen. John A. *McAllen History.* Privately printed (n.d.).

Nevin, Alfred. *Churches of the Valley.* Philadelphia: Joseph M. Wilson, 1852.

Parks, J. W. *Libonia.* Chambersburg, PA: Kittochinny Historical Society, Volume XV, Kerr Printing Company, 1970.

Presbytery of Carlisle. *Centennial Memorial Presbytery, Volumes I and II.* Harrisburg, PA: Meyers Publishing and Printing, 1889.

Ruhl, Lottie Kent. *Our Town: Fannettsburg.* Privately printed (n.d.).

Shearer, Fred. *Lower Path Valley Presbyterian Churches.* Chambersburg, PA: Kittochtinny Historical Society, Volume XV, 1970.

Shearer, Fred. *Lower Path Valley Church, Minister, Rev. A.A. McGinley.* Chambersburg, PA: Kittochtinny Historical Society, Volume XVI, 1978.

Thompson, Peggy. "National Seed Company Had Local Origin," *News Chronicle* (Shippensburg, PA), 1990 (issue unknown).

Vocke, Mary. Interviews with Alice Meloy, 2009–2011.

Witherow, Lucy. *Carrick Furnace: A Legacy.* Chambersburg, PA: Kittochtinny Historical Society, Volume XX, Windmill Publications, 1998.

———. *The McConnell Letters (1813-1860).* Privately printed. (n.d.).

Woods, T. B. *The Old Mills of Franklin County.* Chambersburg, PA.: Kittochtinny Historical Society, Volume X, 1923.

CHAPTER NINE

Bates, Samuel. *History of Franklin County, Pennsylvania,* 1975. First published 1887.

Beers, D. G. *Atlas of Franklin County, Pennsylvania,* 1868.

Diehl, Samuel. *An Old Home in Path Valley.* Chambersburg, PA: Kittochtinny Historical Society, Volume XIV, Craft Press, 1963.

Harris, Fred. *The Harris Family History.* Privately printed (n.d.).

Jones, Bertha. *History of Concord Circuit.* Privately printed (n.d.).

Linn, George Wilds. *History of a Fragment of the Clan Linn.* Lebanon, PA: privately printed, 1906.

Little, Oscar. *History of Concord.* Privately printed (n.d.).

Maser, Frederick E. *Methodism in Central Pennsylvania.* Harrisburg, PA: The United Methodist Church of Central Pennsylvania, Annual Conference Publication, 1971.

McMullen, Sue. "Path and Amberson Valley News," *News Chronicle* (Shippensburg, PA).

Miller, Mary Grace: "History of the Methodist Church" (unpublished manuscript and notes).

Shearer, Fred W. *Lodge Number 74 Free and Accepted Masons, Concord, Franklin County.* Chambersburg, PA: The Kittochtinny Historical Society, Volume XVI, Mercersburg Printing, 1978.

Sloane, Eric. *American Yesterday.* New York: Thomas Y. Crowell, 1956.

Stewart, Reid W. *A History of Scottish Dissenting Presbyterianism in Franklin County, Pennsylvania.* Apollo, PA: Closson Press, 1987.

Fragments of undated historical documents were found in old merchant log books, scrapbooks, newspapers, and correspondence that cannot be attributed to specific individuals.

Chapter Ten

Kayhoe, Donald E. *Path Valley Geography, History, William Penn, The Indians, The Settler, Doylesburg Cemeteries, Fannett Families, Genealogy, New and Revised.* Privately printed, 2001.

McClure, Millie Beale, and Eleanor Work. *History of the Middle Tuscarora Presbyterian Church 1792–1942.* Privately printed (n.d.).

Chapter Eleven

Beers, D. G. *Atlas of Franklin County Pennsylvania,* 1868.

Camp, D. I., and J. Warren Kaufman. *History of Path Valley Presbyterian Churches,* 1916.

Norcross, George. *Centennial Memorial Presbytery of Carlisle, Volume I.* Carlisle, PA: Carlisle Presbytery, 1889.

Chapter Twelve

Crouse, Clyde. Interviews with Alice Meloy, Dry Run and Doylesburg, PA, 1967–1976.

Crouse, Dorothy. Interviews with Alice Meloy, Spring Run, PA, 1970–1978.

Crouse, Eleanor. Interviews with Alice Meloy, Dry Run and Doylesburg, PA, 1960–1980.

Crouse, Robert. Interviews with Alice Meloy, Dry Run and Doylesburg, PA, 1960–1980.

McCartney, Bess. Interviews with Alice Meloy, Dry Run, PA, 1962–1978.

Stewart, Mary Ferguson. Interviews with Alice Meloy, Dry Run, PA, 1935–1953.

Chapter Thirteen

Alexander, Ted, and W. P. Conrad. *When War Passed This Way.* Shippensburg, PA: Greencastle Bicentennial Publication, Beidel Printing House, Inc., 1982.

Alexander, Ted. *The One Hundred and Twenty-Sixth Pennsylvania.* Shippensburg, PA: Beidel Printing House, 1984.

Appel, John W. *The Light of Parnell.* Philadelphia: Heidelberg Press, 1916.

Blockson, Charles. *The Underground Railroad in Pennsylvania.* Jacksonville, NC: Flame International, 1981.

Catton, Bruce. *The Army of the Potomac.* New York: Doubleday and Co., 1951.

———. *A Stillness at Appomattox.* New York: Doubleday and Co., 1953.

Conrad, William P. *Franklin's First Nine Month Soldier.* Chambersburg, PA: Kittochtinny Historical Society, Volume XVII, 1981.

Fogelsanger, Conrad. *The Year 1863 of the Civil War as It Pertained to Franklin County.* Chambersburg, PA: Kittochtinny Historical Society, Volume XIV, 1963.

Gallagher, Gary. *The Annuals of the Civil War.* New York: Da Capo Press, 1994.

Harbaugh, James F. "Mercersburg in War Times," *Mercersburg Journal* (Mercersburg, PA), 2002.

Hoke, Jacob. *The Great Invasion.* Gettysburg, PA: Stan Clark Military Books, 1959.

Hoover, Lee. *Civil War Camps In and About Chambersburg.* Chambersburg, PA: Kittochtinny Historical Society, Volume XIV, Craft Press, 1963.

Jacobs, M. *Notes on the Rebel Invasion of Maryland and Pennsylvania.* Philadelphia: J. B. Lippincott and Co., 1864.

Long, E. B., with Barbara Long. *The Civil War Day by Day Almanac 1861–1865.* New York: Doubleday and Co., 1971.

McClellan, Henry B. *I Rode with Jeb Stuart.* New York: Da Capo Press, 1994.

McPherson, James M. *Battle Cry of Freedom: The Civil War Era.* New York: Ballantine Books, 1988.

Nesbitt, Mark. *35 Days to Gettysburg: The Campaign Diaries of Two American Enemies.* Harrisburg, PA: Stackpole Books, 1992.

Omwake, Stanley. *Franklin County through Confederate Eyes.* Chambersburg, PA: The Kittochtinny Historical Society, Volume XIV, 1963.

Schlesinger, Arthur M. *The Almanac of American History.* New York: Perigee Books, 1983.

Schneck, B. S. *The Burning of Chambersburg, Pennsylvania.* Philadelphia: Lindsay and Blakiston, 1864.

Shaara, Jeff. *Gods and Generals.* New York: Ballantine Books, 1996.

Smith, Page. *Trial by Force: A People's History of the Civil War and Reconstruction, Volume 5.* New York: Penguin Books, 1982.

Stackpole, Edward J. *The Fredericksburg Campaign.* Harrisburg, PA: Stackpole Books, 1992.

Stampp, Kenneth M. *America in 1857.* Oxford, UK: Oxford University Press, 1990.

Stern, Philip Van Doren. *Soldier Life in the Union and Confederate Armies.* New York: Bonanza Books, 1961.

Switala, William J. *Underground Railroad in Pennsylvania.* Mechanicsburg, PA: Stackpole Books, 2001.

Trudeau, Noah Andre. *Bloody Roads South.* New York: Ballantine Books, 1989.

———. *The Last Citadel: Petersburg, Virginia, June 1864–April 1865.* Baton Rouge: Louisiana State University Press, 1991.

Ward, George W. *History of the Second Pennsylvania Veteran Heavy Artillery, 12th Regiment Pennsylvania Volunteers from 1861–1866, including the Provisional Second Penns's Heavy Artillery.* Philadelphia: George W. Ward, Printer, 1904.

Wheeler, Richard. *Witness to Gettysburg.* New York: Penguin Books, 1987.

Wiley, Samuel. *Biography and History, Schuykill County, PA.* Philadelphia: Rush, West and Co., 1893.

Wills, Garry. *Lincoln at Gettyburg.* New York: Simon and Schuster, 1992.

Winik, Jay. *April 1865.* New York: HarperCollins Publishers, 2001.

WA